THE ROYAL HOR`
PRACTI(

D0785196

TREES FOR
SMALL GARDENS

THE ROYAL HORTICULTURAL SOCIETY
PRACTICAL GUIDES

TREES FOR
SMALL GARDENS

ALLEN J. COOMBES

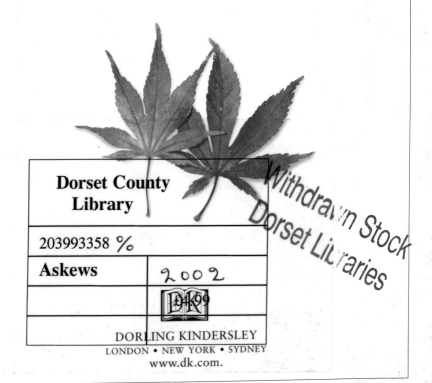

DORLING KINDERSLEY
LONDON • NEW YORK • SYDNEY
www.dk.com.

LONDON, NEW YORK, MUNICH, MELBOURNE, DELHI

PRODUCED FOR DORLING KINDERSLEY BY STUDIO CACTUS, 13 Southgate Street, Winchester, Hampshire

PROJECT EDITOR Polly Boyd
PROJECT ART EDITOR Ann Thompson

SERIES EDITOR Gillian Roberts
SERIES ART EDITOR Stephen Josland

SENIOR MANAGING EDITOR Mary-Clare Jerram
MANAGING ART EDITOR Lee Griffiths

DTP DESIGNER Louise Paddick

PRODUCTION CONTROLLER Mandy Inness

First published in Great Britain in 2000
Reprinted 2002
by Dorling Kindersley Limited,
80 Strand, London WC2R 0RL

A Penguin Company

A CIP catalogue for this book is available from the British Library.
ISBN 0 7513 47213

Reproduced by Colourscan, Singapore
Printed and bound by Star Standard Industries, Singapore

See our complete catalogue at
www.dk.com

CONTENTS

WHY HAVE TREES IN THE GARDEN?

WHAT IS A TREE?

TREES ARE GENERALLY THE LARGEST and most prominent features in the garden. They are usually defined as woody plants that will grow on a single stem to at least 5–6m (15–20ft) tall, whereas a shrub, which is also woody, is normally lower growing, with several or many stems from the base. However, there is not always a clear division between the two; some plants that we think of as trees can be shrubby, while some shrubs can develop a tree-like habit.

TREES IN SMALL GARDENS

While many trees are vast, a great number are more modest in stature, and are ideally suited to small gardens. Most of the trees featured in this book reach only about 10m (30ft) tall; however, some taller, narrow trees are also included, since they are useful where the width rather than the height of tree is the limiting factor. Many trees grow well in containers (*see pp.32–35*), and are ideal for enlivening paved areas such as roof terraces, basements, and courtyards.

BENEFITS OF TREES

• Trees are highly ornamental plants. They add form, height, and structure to the garden.
• They can be used to create focal points, to highlight or hide parts of the garden, or to frame or obscure the outside world.
• Trees are long-lived, and they require little attention once they are established.
• They encourage wildlife in their branches, on their bark, and on the ground beneath.
• Trees can provide shelter and shade.

SPRING-FLOWERING CHERRY *Throughout the year, trees bring colour, form, and substance to the garden: many offer glorious flowers and foliage in spring and summer (here,* Prunus 'Hally Jolivette'*), magnificent colour in autumn, and striking, bare-branched silhouettes in winter. Trees make a bold statement in their own right; they also complement other plantings and create sheltered or shady areas in which to grow a range of plants.*

◀ AUTUMN GLORY *Ablaze with colour, this cherry is offset dramatically by the bluish green conifer.*

TREES IN PLANTING PLANS

The size and layout of your garden will determine the number of trees to plant and their positions. In a very small garden, there may be only enough space for one tree and little choice of where to plant it. As the size of garden increases, so do the possibilities of design using trees.

Some trees make excellent specimen plants. They may form an eye-catching focal point, or may highlight an area of the garden by drawing attention to it. Many combine well with other plantings. The

> Trees may be used to highlight or hide certain areas of the garden

mixed border – an important feature in many small gardens – combines both woody and herbaceous plants. Here, trees combine happily with shrubs and perennials, and lend height, structure, and year-round interest to any display.

It may be necessary to change the planting around a tree as it grows, using sun-loving plants around a young tree and

BRIGHTENING A DARK AREA
Shade-tolerant plants, such as the maple Acer shirasawanum *'Aureum' and* Pittosporum *'Garnettii', can lighten a shady corner.*

changing them for shade-tolerant ones as the tree spreads and creates more shade. An alternative approach is to grow an upright tree that will cast little shadow, for example the cherry *Prunus* 'Amanogawa' or *Thuja occidentalis* 'Smaragd', or to underplant shrubs that will grow well in both sun and shade, such as *Skimmia ×* *confusa* 'Kew Green' or *Viburnum tinus*.

Before planting a tree, there are various important points to consider that will effect the kind of tree you plant and its position. First, decide whether you wish to retain the view from the garden or to obscure it. Trees can do both effectively: they may conceal a nearby building, or frame a view

A TREE AS A FOCAL POINT
Viewed through an archway in the hedge, this carefully placed crab apple, Malus *'Golden Hornet', is a striking and effective focal point.*

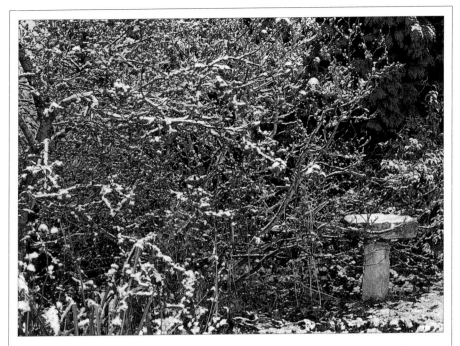

to distant hills. Consider whether you want the tree to divide the garden, creating a screen between two distinct areas, or to draw the eye into another part of it. The tree's ornamental features should also have a bearing on its position. If you are growing a tree for its bark, it needs to be in a reasonably open position where the bark can be seen to best effect, whereas one grown for its spring flowers or autumn

> If space is at a premium, select a tree with two or more seasons of interest

colour could be planted among shade-tolerant shrubs and still get noticed. Never be tempted to plant a tree that will become too large for the site. In the majority of cases, it is impractical as well as undesirable to prune most trees to restrict their size.

In a small garden, avoid planting too many yellow-leaved, variegated, or purple-

YEAR-ROUND INTEREST
Many trees are ornamental over several seasons. The crab apple Malus 'Red Sentinel' *offers spring flowers and fruits into winter.*

leaved trees. While they are useful for highlighting and drawing attention to certain parts of the garden, they can dominate in a central position. Trees with bold foliage or a strong, upright habit are often very effective near buildings.

Where there is space for only one or two trees, the ornamental features are especially important. A wide range of trees have attractions that span two or more seasons – flowers, then autumn colour, and attractive bark, for example – so these are a good choice for very small gardens, where every plant must earn its keep. Many trees are attractive throughout the year. Silver birches, for example, bear their fresh green leaves and catkins in spring, the elegantly drooping foliage in summer turns to yellow in autumn, while the striking white bark is a particularly welcome feature in winter.

SUITING THE TREE TO THE SITE

ALTHOUGH MANY TREES will grow happily in a range of garden conditions, there are those that prefer or even require a certain position or soil type. If you wish to plant a particular tree, ensure that the conditions in your garden are suitable for it to thrive. Remember to take into account practical factors such as space available, exposure to wind, amount of shade, and whether the soil is dry, moist, acidic, or alkaline (*see p.42*).

SUN AND SHADE

Most trees will tolerate a fairly broad range of conditions from full sun to partial shade, and will succeed where they are shaded by a building or other trees for several hours of the day. Others, however, will positively thrive in full sun, flowering and growing the better for it. Most trees with coloured or variegated foliage are at their best if given plenty of light, but they do not necessarily need full sun all day. If grown in too much shade, their foliage tends to become greener and less interesting.

With some trees, it is a case of balancing the plant's requirements. The very beautiful beech, *Fagus sylvatica* 'Aurea Pendula', for

▲ SUN-LOVING BUDDLEJA
Buddleja alternifolia, *grown as a weeping standard, is an ideal small tree for a sunny position. Fewer fragrant, early summer flowers would be produced in a shadier site.*

◄ SHADE-TOLERANT STYRAX
Naturally a woodland species, the graceful, spreading Japanese snowbell tree (Styrax japonicus) will flower well and produce good autumn colour in shady sites in the garden.

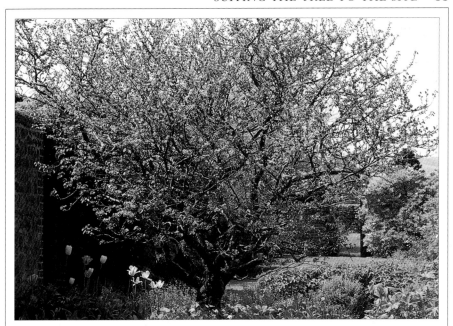

example, has bright yellow foliage, which may burn in full sun when it emerges; it is therefore best given a bright position among other trees. In the case of the sorrel tree (*Oxydendrum arboreum*) and *Stewartia pseudocamellia*, both full sun and a moist soil are needed. If these conditions are difficult to provide in the garden, then such trees are best grown in partial shade, where the soil is likely to be moister.

> Most trees with variegated leaves perform best in plenty of light

Some trees grow well in light shade, either under larger trees, or where they are prevented from receiving sun for most of the day, in the shadow of a building for example. The area beneath a large, densely leafy tree may be very dry as well as shady, so grow trees that tolerate dry, shady sites, such as hollies (*Ilex*) and yews (*Taxus*), or add a soil improver before planting.

SUN-WORSHIPPING CERCIS
The Judas tree (Cercis siliquastrum) *originates in the hot, sunny climate of the eastern Mediterranean. If given a site in full sun, it bears a profusion of pink flowers in spring.*

WHAT TREE WHERE?

TREES FOR SUNNY SITES
Cordyline australis
Cupressus
Elaeagnus angustifolia
Ficus carica
Franklinia alatamaha
Koelreuteria paniculata
Pyrus
Syringa

TREES FOR SHADY SITES
Acer (most)
Aesculus × *neglecta* 'Erythroblastos'
Amelanchier
Carpinus
Ilex
Photinia
Styrax japonicus
Taxus baccata

TREE SHAPES

THE SHAPE OF A TREE has a major impact, especially on a small garden. For most of the year, a tree will not be in flower or fruit, or showing autumn colour, so it is the form that, to a great extent, sets the garden's mood and style. When selecting a tree, always consider the shape as well as the ultimate height. If horizontal space is restricted, a conical or columnar tree is best, since they occupy less space than a spreading tree of the same height.

COLUMNAR TREES

Trees defined as "columnar" are upright, with an ultimate height greater than their spread; the crown is more or less parallel-sided. The broadest of these, which may be only a little taller than wide, are often called "broadly columnar", the narrowest are classified as "narrowly columnar".

The columnar habit has distinct advantages in small gardens. A tree of relatively narrow spread takes up less space, enabling it to be grown in more confined areas than a wider-spreading tree. In addition, the fact that a columnar tree creates less shade allows a greater range of plants to be grown beneath it.

One of the great characteristics of columnar trees is that they create a bold statement, which makes them excellent as focal points or specimen trees. With their distinctive shape, they stand out beautifully in the garden and complement both trees and shrubs of more spreading habits.

△ LOLLIPOP-SHAPED SPECIMEN
The hornbeam Carpinus betulus 'Columnaris' *makes a strong, bold statement in the garden. These trees are narrowly columnar when young, becoming more rounded with age.*

| BROADLY COLUMNAR | NARROWLY COLUMNAR | BROADLY CONICAL | NARROWLY CONICAL |

CONICAL TREES

Conical trees are similar to columnar trees in that they are upright, with a height that is greater than their spread. They differ, however, in that their crowns are not parallel-sided but instead are tapered to a point. As with columnar trees, the ratio of height to spread varies considerably, with the broadest termed "broadly conical", and the more slender and spire-like classified as "narrowly conical". Because of their distinctive habit, conical trees make good specimen trees or focal points, and are also

> In confined spaces,
> upright forms are better
> than spreading shapes

effective in mixed borders, where they provide interesting, contrasting shapes.

Narrow trees can often be used effectively in groups or pairs. A group of three slender trees, such as *Pinus sylvestris* 'Fastigiata', makes a bold feature in the garden, and can occupy less space than a single spreading tree. Narrow trees can also be used to flank a path or gateway, with little danger of obstruction as they grow. Alternatively, they can frame a view from the garden or, together with other trees, form an effective component of a screen.

▲ CONICAL CONIFER
Chamaecyparis obtusa *'Crippsii', a good specimen tree, is tall and slender when young, but becomes broader and more open with age.*

ROUNDED TO BROADLY SPREADING

WEEPING

◄ TREE SHAPES
Trees come in a wide range of forms. The shape of the tree you choose will influence which plants you can grow beneath.

ROUNDED TO SPREADING TREES

Trees that are defined as "rounded to spreading" have a crown that is generally broader than it is tall. These are very attractive in form, but they take up more horizontal space than upright trees.

When choosing a tree, always check on its eventual shape. In the nursery, many young

> Many young trees are upright, but become wide spreading with age

trees have an upright habit, which several years later will start to spread widely. Take care at planting to ensure that trees of a spreading habit will not later encroach on other plants or structures. Also, consider

WEEPING CHERRY
The elegant habit of this cherry, Prunus pendula *'Pendula Rosea', is offset by a dark background of upright evergreens, which form an excellent foil for the pink flowers.*

your choice of plants beneath the tree. Spreading trees produce the largest areas of shade, some light and dappled, others dense. Those that create dense shade are useful for screening and naturally provide the ideal conditions for growing shade-loving plants (*see p.37*).

WEEPING TREES

Weeping trees are usually spreading in habit, with pendulous branches, although some, such as the beech *Fagus sylvatica* 'Aurea Pendula', retain a narrow form.

One kind of weeping tree is particularly useful for small gardens. Plants that would naturally grow as low, spreading mounds close to the ground are instead grafted on top of a stem at about 1.2–2m (4–6ft) tall. When grown in this way, the normally creeping shoots arch gracefully to the ground, creating a weeping tree. Examples of some good weeping standards include *Caragana arborescens* 'Pendula', *Cotoneaster* 'Hybridus Pendulus', and the cherry *Prunus* 'Kiku-shidare-zakura'.

◄ BROADLY CONICAL
Conical trees, such as the crab apple Malus tschonoskii, *stand out well among other trees of contrasting shapes.*

▼ SHRUB GROWN AS A TREE
The willow Salix integra *'Hakuro-nishiki' is a shrub that is usually grafted on a stem to make a small tree.*

TREES WITH DISTINCTIVE SHAPES

BROADLY COLUMNAR
Acer palmatum 'Shishigashira'
Aesculus × *neglecta* 'Erythroblastos'
Eucryphia glutinosa
Lagerstroemia indica
Prunus 'Spire'

NARROWLY COLUMNAR
Calocedrus decurrens 'Berrima Gold'
Juniperus chinensis 'Spartan'
Picea pungens f. *glauca*
Pinus sylvestris 'Fastigiata'
Prunus 'Amanogawa'

BROADLY SPREADING
Albizia julibrissin f. *rosea*
Catalpa bignonioides 'Aurea'
Genista aetnensis
Prunus × *subhirtella* 'Autumnalis'
Sorbus sargentiana

BROADLY CONICAL
Cornus macrophylla
Ligustrum lucidum
Magnolia macrophylla
Malus tschonoskii
Trochodendron aralioides

NARROWLY CONICAL
Abies koreana
Betula populifolia
Cupressus arizonica 'Pyramidalis'
Juniperus chinensis 'Aurea'
Pyrus calleryana 'Chanticleer'

WEEPING
Buddleja alternifolia
Caragana arborescens 'Pendula'
Ilex aquifolium 'Argentea Marginata Pendula'
Malus 'Royal Beauty'
Prunus 'Kiku-shidare-zakura'

SCREENS AND BOUNDARIES

TREES FREQUENTLY NEED to be useful as well as ornamental. One of their prime functions is to screen the garden from the sights and sounds of the outside world. Trees are also good for "dividing" the garden, separating a vegetable plot from an ornamental area, for example, or concealing an unsightly structure. In exposed gardens, a boundary screen is particularly beneficial, since it gives protection, enabling more delicate plants to be grown.

SCREENING WITH TREES

In large gardens, a traditional boundary screen consists of a belt of large trees planted around the perimeter of the garden; the trees are chosen to blend in well with the surrounding countryside so that they do not appear obtrusive, while more ornamental plantings are usually reserved for areas closer to the house. In smaller gardens, however, where space is at a premium, boundary plantings need to be both functional and decorative.

Hedges composed of single species of privet (*Ligustrum*) and cypresses (*Chamaecyparis*, × *Cupressocyparis*, and *Cupressus*) are often used for boundary plantings in small gardens. While these are functional, they often lack interest and provide little ornamental appeal. They can also require considerable maintenance, particularly when composed of fast-growing plants such as Leyland cypress (× *Cupressocyparis leylandii*).

As an alternative to the traditional hedge, trees can provide effective, varied, and decorative screens, especially when combined with ornamental shrubs. A single carefully placed specimen can hide an unsightly view, building, or neighbour's window, while a line of mixed trees will quickly seclude the garden and provide interest throughout the year.

PRIVATE REFUGE
Using ornamental trees ensures a screen is attractive as well as useful. Here, a normally large tree, Acer platanoides 'Drummondii', *has been used to enclose part of a garden, obscuring a greenhouse to the rear. Grown so close to each other, these maples would soon shade this area, so they need to be cut back regularly to restrict their size and keep them compact.*

◀ A SPLASH OF COLOUR
An existing boundary planting of evergreens can be enlivened considerably by planting an occasional deciduous tree in front. The bright autumn colour of these maples, Acer capillipes *and A. palmatum, is an effective foil to the dark evergreen foliage.*

▼ CREATING A BOUNDARY
A boundary composed of a mixture of ornamental trees and shrubs – deciduous and evergreen – is both functional and attractive. Here, Acer negundo 'Flamingo', *a maple with variegated leaves, stands out among the other trees.*

CHOOSING THE RIGHT TREES

For screens and boundary plantings, select trees that are reasonably fast growing, hardy, and will withstand exposure if necessary. To create a dense screen, avoid trees that are very open in habit, such as *Genista aetnensis*, and those that are relatively late into leaf, such as *Catalpa*, *Gleditsia*, and *Robinia*, since for much of the year these will be without foliage.

> Trees can conceal eyesores and provide privacy in the garden

Combining deciduous and evergreen trees ensures seasonal variety as well as a certain degree of privacy. For additional interest, use trees of various shapes, such as an upright holly (*Ilex*) with a spreading hawthorn (*Crataegus*). A narrow habit is particularly effective and useful where there is limited space, for example when a dividing screen is required in a small garden: trees such as hollies and *Pittosporum tenuifolium* are ideal.

SUITABLE TREES

DECIDUOUS
Acer platanoides 'Globosum'
Carpinus betulus 'Columnaris'
Crataegus laevigata
Malus cultivars
Sorbus aria 'Lutescens'

EVERGREEN
Arbutus unedo
Ilex × *altaclerensis*/*I. aquifolium* cultivars
Ligustrum lucidum cultivars
Photinia × *fraseri* cultivars
Pittosporum tenuifolium

CREATING SHADE AND SHELTER

EXPOSED AND OPEN AREAS of the garden can be inhospitable, since they are often cold and windy in winter and hot and dry in summer. However, with one or two carefully placed trees, you can create a very pleasant shady or sheltered spot. Trees provide ideal conditions for an underplanting of shade-loving shrubs and perennials; they also offer a canopy under which you can sit and relax, protected to a great extent from the elements.

LIGHT AND DENSE SHADE

All trees create shade, but the amount of shade they give varies considerably depending on the kind of tree. Shape is a key factor: spreading trees cast a greater area of shade than conical or columnar ones, for example. The depth of shade, whether it is deep or light and dappled, depends on the density of a tree's foliage. For a woodland-style planting of shade-loving shrubs and perennials, a spreading tree provides the most suitable conditions.

The kinds of plants that can be used beneath a tree will depend on the space available; again, this is greatly influenced by the tree's shape, as well as the height at which it branches. A weeping tree, with branches sweeping to the ground, will give little scope for underplanting, whereas there is space to grow many shrubs and perennials beneath a rounded or spreading

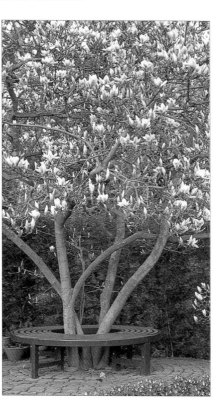

▲ SHADY RETREAT
A mature Magnolia × soulangeana *is highlighted by a functional and ornamental circular bench, making it an inviting place to sit, either beneath the flowers in spring or the dense, leafy shade in summer.*

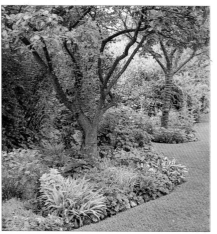

◀ SHADE-LOVING PLANTING
Tree canopies provide shelter for many shade-loving plants. Here, a Victoria plum tree filters the sun from a planting of woodland perennials, including hostas and corydalis.

tree (*see p.37*). If you wish to grow plants that require light but benefit from shelter, such as rhododendrons, azaleas, camellias, and *Pieris*, two or more trees planted at about one-and-a-half to two times their spread apart will provide suitable conditions. Position the plants towards the edge of the canopy.

> For a large area of shade, use spreading rather than conical or columnar trees

There is more flexibility in the type of tree you can choose if the area beneath it is not planted but instead houses a bench or circular seat, for example. An attractive seating arrangement also serves to draw attention to a specimen tree. Established trees may also be used as supports, for hammocks or swings in the shade.

TREES TO CREATE SHADE

DAPPLED SHADE
Albizia julibrissin f. *rosea*
Genista aetnensis
Koelreuteria paniculata
Prunus × *subhirtella* 'Autumnalis'
Styrax japonicus

DENSE SHADE
Acer davidii, A. rufinerve
Cornus macrophylla
Crataegus laevigata, C. × *lavallei* 'Carrierei'
Laburnum × *watereri* 'Vossii'
Magnolia obovata, M. × *soulangeana*
Malus 'Golden Hornet', *M. hupehensis*
Photinia × *fraseri*
Prunus sargentii

A PLACE FOR REST AND SHELTER
These two crab apples could have shaded a woodland planting, but they are equally valuable for creating a sheltered resting place on a warm, sunny day.

FEATURE TREES

WHILE SOME TREES form a functional backdrop in a garden, such as those planted on a boundary, others take centre stage, placed at strategic points to display their striking ornamental characteristics to best effect. Feature trees can be used as focal points in their own right, or may serve to highlight a particular setting. They may also lead the eye to another area, frame a distant view, or mark the division between two distinct areas of a garden.

USING FEATURE TREES

There is a diverse range of small trees suitable as feature specimens. Although the kind of tree to plant is, to a large extent, a matter of personal taste, there are several criteria to take into account when making your choice. A feature tree should have one or more bold characteristics, and it must be sufficiently impressive to stand on its own, either contrasting with or complementing nearby plantings. It must also be of a suitable size for its position; if a tree is too large, or too small, it will not achieve the desired effect.

Many trees planted as specimens are chosen for their flowers, fruit, or foliage, but a strong shape adds greatly to the impact of a tree. For this reason, many weeping trees make ideal features. Trees with a strong, upright habit are also useful, particularly when they have the added bonus of ornamental foliage.

> A feature tree must have bold characteristics and, preferably, a strong shape

Feature trees can occupy many positions in the garden, provided they are not hidden among other plants. Use them to highlight a particular area, or to draw the eye to a far corner. They can also be used effectively

BOLD BORDER FEATURE
The extremely pendulous habit and bold purple leaves make the weeping purple beech (Fagus sylvatica 'Purpurea Pendula') an eye-catching feature in this border. This specimen has been grafted low down to make a small tree, but these beeches are frequently taller, with branches weeping to the ground and mushroom-shaped heads. A tree this size makes a good feature only because it is in scale with the surrounding plants in the border; it would be ineffective in a more open position.

SUITABLE TREES

DECIDUOUS

Acer pseudoplatanus
'Brilliantissimum'
Betula utilis var.
jacquemontii
Catalpa bignonioides
'Aurea'
Cornus controversa
'Variegata'
Fagus sylvatica 'Dawyck
Gold'
Pyrus calleryana
'Chanticleer'

EVERGREEN

Arbutus × *andrachnoides*
Cupressus arizonica
'Pyramidalis'
Ilex aquifolium/I. ×
altaclerensis cultivars
Ligustrum lucidum
'Excelsum Superbum'
Photinia × *fraseri*
Picea pungens f. *glauca*
Trachycarpus fortunei

◀ STRIKING FOCAL POINT
A weeping silver pear, Pyrus
salicifolia *'Pendula', with its
lower branches removed, has
a prominent position in the
centre of intersecting paths.*

to add ornament to garden structures, such
as a flight of steps or a pond. A carefully
placed pair of trees can be used to frame
an attractive view.

Feature trees are often placed in the
centre of a lawn, although this is not
always the best position for them. Consider
instead planting one at the side, perhaps
either next to a patio or terrace, where it
can cast its shade, or in or close to an
adjacent border, where its strong shape will
draw the eye from the expanse of green. In
borders or island beds, trees provide a
useful contrast to lower-growing perennials
and shrubs, such as heathers and dwarf
conifers, adding often-needed height.

▲ LAWN SPECIMEN
*A feature tree placed to the side of a lawn
often makes more impact than one positioned
in the centre, as is shown by this* Prunus ×
subhirtella *'Autumnalis'.*

MULTI-SEASONAL TREES

IN MANY CASES, trees have only one outstanding ornamental feature – flowers, autumn colour, or fruits for example. However, there is a good selection of those that have a number of decorative qualities that span two or more seasons. These trees are known as "multi-seasonal", and they are invaluable in small gardens. If you only have space in the garden for one or two trees, it is particularly important that they provide interest for most, if not all, of the year.

TREES FOR ALL SEASONS

Flowers are frequently one of the main reasons for choosing a tree. However, a tree that may be striking in bloom for a few weeks can often look relatively dull the rest of the year. When choosing a tree for multi-seasonal interest, other ornamental features must be taken into account, such as fruit, foliage, bark and stems, and habit.

Trees with eye-catching flowers as well as ornamental fruits include the crab apples (*Malus*) and rowans (*Sorbus*). Those with attractive flowers and good autumn colour include the cherries *Prunus* 'Okame' and *P. sargentii*. Some trees, such as many rowans and *Photinia villosa*, have attractive flowers and fruit, and good autumn colour.

Interesting bark is a very important aspect of many multi-seasonal trees, since it will be an attraction throughout the year. Combine ornamental bark with other features, such as flowers in *Stewartia pseudocamellia*, which also has good autumn colour. Some trees have specific winter features that add to their value,

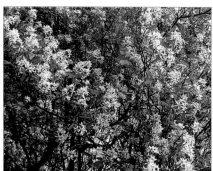

▶ SPRING FLOWERS
Amelanchier lamarckii *starts its show with profuse white flowers in mid-spring, accompanied by attractive young foliage, bronze with silky hairs.*

▲ AUTUMN COLOUR
After the long display of flowers, purple-black fruits, and spring and summer foliage, Amelanchier lamarckii *exhibits its magnificent bright autumn colours.*

extending the season of interest. The maple *Acer pensylvanicum* 'Erythrocladum', for example, has brilliant pink winter shoots combined with yellow streaked bark, as well as yellow autumn leaves. Evergreens are invaluable in the multi-seasonal garden,

> Multi-seasonal trees must have two or preferably more seasons of interest

but they should not be used exclusively, since their foliage shows less variation than deciduous trees. However, some evergreens are multi-seasonal trees in their own right. *Arbutus* × *andrachnoides* has attractive bark as well as flowers and fruit, while many hollies (*Ilex*) are useful for their often variegated leaves and their colourful fruits.

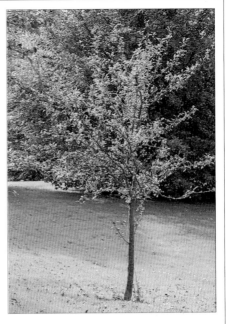

▲ CRAB APPLE IN AUTUMN
Many of the crab apples are attractive over more than one season. Malus 'Golden Hornet' is best known for its autumn fruits, but it also bears white flowers from pink buds in spring.

◀ CHERRY IN WINTER
Trees grown primarily for their bark, such as Prunus serrula, are a particularly welcome sight in winter. This cherry also has bowl-shaped white flowers in spring, followed by cherry-like fruits, and yellow autumn leaves.

MULTI-SEASONAL TREES

Acer (snake-bark maples, *see p.62*)
Amelanchier
Cornus (many)
Cotoneaster 'Hybridus Pendulus'
Crataegus crus-galli, C. persimilis 'Prunifolia'
Eucryphia glutinosa
Franklinia alatamaha
Malus
Photinia × *fraseri*
Prunus 'Okame'
Pyrus calleryana 'Chanticleer'
Sorbus

TREES FOR FLOWERS OR FRUITS

ALL TREES PRODUCE FLOWERS, and while these are sometimes insignificant, many trees are grown specifically for their spectacular, occasionally fragrant, blooms. Flowers provide a relatively brief display; if you have space for only a few trees, choose those that also produce attractive fruits to prolong the season of interest. In a small garden, where trees are viewed at close quarters, even tiny flowers can be highly ornamental, such as those of maples (*Acer*), the hanging catkins of birches (*Betula*), or the dark, honey-scented flowers of *Pittosporum*.

EARLY OFFERINGS

Most trees produce their flowers in spring, including some of the most popular trees for blossom, such as the cherries (*Prunus*). These range from the early-flowering forms of the cherry plums (*P. cerasifera*) to the Japanese cherries, some of which, such as *P.* 'Shirofugen', flower late in the season. Spring is also

> Trees with striking fruits as well as flowers are ideal for small gardens

the flowering time for most of the crab apples (*Malus*), many of which have the additional bonus of ornamental fruits.

Magnolias also offer excellent flowers in spring. *M.* × *soulangeana* is a popular choice, but more unusual are the forms of *M.* × *loebneri*, such as 'Leonard Messel', with starry pink flowers. There are also the summer-flowering magnolias, including *M. obovata*, with headily fragrant flowers and large red fruit clusters in autumn.

The flowering dogwoods (*Cornus*) have tiny, insignificant flowers, but very showy bracts surrounding them. Among the most spectacular of these is *C.* 'Norman Hadden', which provides two months' display from early to midsummer as the bracts change from creamy white to deep pink, followed in autumn by unusual strawberry-like fruits.

FRUIT CLUSTERS IN AUTUMN
This hawthorn, Crataegus persimilis *'Prunifolia', bears attractive white flowers in late spring. Another great season of interest is autumn, when the clusters of bright red fruits combine with the colouring foliage to produce a stunning display.*

▲ SPRING SPLENDOUR
The large, showy white flowers of Magnolia salicifolia *'Wada's Memory' cover the tree in spring.*

◄ GOLDEN SHOWER
In spring, the pendulous yellow flower clusters of Laburnum × watereri *'Vossii' are always a spectacular sight.*

LATE ATTRACTIONS

As summer progresses, the number of trees flowering becomes fewer, but there are still some that are at their best at this time. *Eucryphia glutinosa* and *Genista aetnensis* are examples of fine flowering trees for late summer, while *Albizia julibrissin* and *Koelreuteria paniculata* take the display towards autumn, the latter developing ornamental pods after the yellow flowers fade. The white flowers of *Aralia elata* are often produced as the leaves colour. Numerous fruiting trees are at their best in autumn, such as the crab apples and stag's horn sumach (*Rhus typhina*), many with fruits that persist into winter. Some flowers are even produced in winter, namely those of the strawberry trees (*Arbutus*), which bear their red fruits at the same time, and *Prunus* × *subhirtella*, which blooms from autumn to spring in mild weather.

RECOMMENDED TREES

TREES FOR FLOWERS

Cornus (flowering dogwoods, *see p.65*)
Halesia monticola
Koelreuteria paniculata
Laburnum × *watereri* 'Vossii'
Magnolia (many)
Malus (many)
Prunus (many)
Stewartia pseudocamellia

TREES FOR FRUITS

Abies koreana
Cornus 'Norman Hadden'
Crataegus (several, not double forms)
Ilex (many)
Koelreuteria paniculata
Malus (many)
Rhus typhina
Sorbus (many)

TREES FOR FOLIAGE

FLOWERS AND FRUITS are frequently a tree's most striking assets, yet they provide interest for only a few weeks. Foliage, however, is a much longer-lasting feature, which should always be a prime consideration when choosing a tree. Leaves offer an immense diversity of sizes, shapes, colours, and textures. If you have space for several trees, combine a variety of leaf types, both deciduous and evergreen, to create attractive, contrasting effects.

DECIDUOUS TREES

Trees with variegated or coloured leaves are often very attractive, especially when contrasted with green foliage. However, they should be used sparingly, particularly in a small garden, where too many of them may overwhelm other plants. For seasonal variety, use trees that have variously coloured foliage in spring or autumn but are green-leaved much of the time in between, such as *Acer pseudoplatanus*

'Brilliantissimum', which has excellent early pink leaves. Many trees are grown for their attractively shaped leaves. The maples (*Acer*), for example, have very ornamental leaves, which develop good autumn colour, while *Alnus glutinosa* 'Imperialis' combines deeply cut foliage with a graceful habit. Trees with large, bold leaves are also effective, such as those of the fig tree (*Ficus carica*) or *Aralia elata*, which also colour well in autumn.

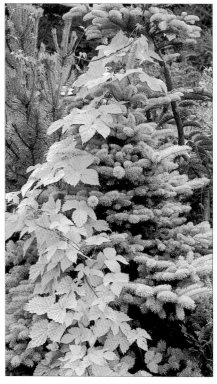

▲ PINKISH HUES
The striking pinkish spring foliage of Aesculus × neglecta *'Erythroblastos' offers an outstanding but rather short-lived display of colour.*

▶ LEAFY CONTRAST
Picea pungens f. glauca *provides a good evergreen backdrop for the climbing golden-leaved hop,* Humulus lupulus *'Aureus'.*

▲ FRESH GREEN MAPLE
Maples, like this Acer
shirasawanum *'Aureum',
shown here in late spring,
provide colourful foliage as
well as interesting leaf shapes.*

◄ SEASONAL CHANGES
*Autumn is one of the most
spectacular times for foliage
colour, with many maples,
such as this* Acer triflorum,
turning to shades of red.

EVERGREEN TREES

Evergreens generally show less variation in
their foliage throughout the year than
deciduous trees (exceptions to this include
Pinus sylvestris 'Aurea', with bright yellow
foliage in winter). However, evergreen trees
have the advantage of providing winter
foliage, which can often be used as an
effective background for other plants. The
Irish yew *Taxus baccata* 'Fastigiata', for
example, has dark green foliage that is an
ideal foil to lighter-leaved deciduous trees,
such as the yellow-leaved maple, *Acer
shirasawanum* 'Aureum'. Many evergreens
are also excellent foliage plants in their
own right. The variegated hollies, which
include forms of *Ilex × altaclerensis* and
I. aquifolium, provide both attractive
foliage and fruits, while the yellow-leaved
form of bay laurel (*Laurus nobilis* 'Aurea')
has colourful, aromatic foliage.

FOLIAGE TREES

DECIDUOUS
Acer (many)
Catalpa bignonioides 'Aurea'
Cornus controversa 'Variegata'
Crataegus persimilis 'Prunifolia'
Fagus sylvatica cultivars
Prunus sargentii
Rhus typhina
Sorbus (rowans)

EVERGREEN
Cupressus arizonica 'Pyramidalis'
Ilex (many)
Juniperus chinensis 'Aurea'
Laurus nobilis 'Aurea'
Photinia × fraseri
Pinus sylvestris 'Aurea'
Pittosporum tenuifolium and cultivars
Taxus baccata cultivars

TREES FOR BARK OR SHOOTS

T HE ORNAMENTAL QUALITIES of bark and shoots are often overlooked, yet they
are among the few features that can be appreciated throughout the year.
Tree bark may be beautifully coloured or patterned, or intriguing in texture,
and planting just one of the many trees grown for this effect will add greatly to
the interest in a garden. Attractive bark is particularly valuable as a winter
feature, combining well with trees grown for their ornamental shoots.

ATTRACTIONS OF BARK

The bark of a tree changes with age: as the
trunk grows taller and thickens, the outer
bark must expand to accommodate it. In
some trees, the bark splits into ridges, often
very deep; in others, the bark peels off in
strips or patches, and falls as new bark is
produced to replace it. Both of these
methods of renewal can produce striking
effects, particularly evident in the streaked
stems of the snake-bark maples, the flaking
bark of *Lagerstroemia* and *Stewartia*, and
the peeling trunks of birches (*Betula*) and
Prunus serrula. Some barks have other
ornamental qualities, such as the
prominently spiny stems of *Aralia elata*, or
the fibrous trunk of *Trachycarpus fortunei*.
Trees that are grown for their
bark are best planted in an open
position, so that their attractive trunks are
not obscured by surrounding plants. Close
to a path is ideal, since the tactile as well as
visual qualities of bark may be enjoyed.
Birches make good focal specimens, since
their clean white stems stand out well, even
at a distance, either planted on their own
or with a suitable contrasting background.

Bark may be washed with a damp cloth
(to remove green algae) and touched gently
without causing harm, but never peel off
strips from birches or cherries, since this
will damage the delicate tissues beneath.

▼PAPER-BARK MAPLE
*The attractive peeling, cinnamon-coloured
bark on its trunk and branches places* Acer
griseum *among the most sought-after trees
grown for this feature.*

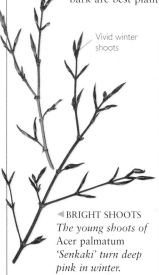

Vivid winter
shoots

◀BRIGHT SHOOTS
The young shoots of
Acer palmatum
'Senkaki' *turn deep
pink in winter.*

◄ STRIPED MAPLE
Attractive green- and white-streaked bark is one of the many subtle qualities of the snake-bark maples, shown here in Acer pensylvanicum.

▲ HIMALAYAN BIRCH
Betula utilis *var.* jacquemontii *is one of the most eye-catching trees grown for bark, especially when set against a darker background.*

TREES WITH STRIKING SHOOTS

Trees grown for their ornamental shoots usually show this feature best in winter. Maples (*Acer*) and willows (*Salix*) predominate. Those used are generally small trees, such as *Acer palmatum* 'Senkaki'. Any large trees are usually coppiced or pollarded to promote vigorous young shoots for winter colour and to restrict the tree's size in order to keep the shoots closer to eye level (*see p.57*).

GOOD CHOICES

TREES FOR ORNAMENTAL BARK
Acer (**A. griseum** and all snake-bark maples, see p.62)
Arbutus × *andrachnoides*
Betula
Lagerstroemia
Luma apiculata
Pinus bungeana
Prunus maackii and *P. serrula*
Stewartia pseudocamellia

TREES FOR COLOURFUL SHOOTS
Acer pensylvanicum 'Erythrocladum'
Salix alba 'Britzensis' and subsp. *vitellina*
Salix 'Erythroflexuosa'

TREES TO ATTRACT WILDLIFE

ALL TREES ATTRACT AND ENCOURAGE wildlife in the garden: birds roost and nest in their branches, and eat their berries, and insects pollinate the flowers (unless they are wind pollinated). Many insects also find a home on the tree or in the soil or detritus beneath, and so attract birds who feed on them. Birds, such as thrushes, are invaluable for controlling garden pests such as snails, slugs, and aphids, provided chemical controls are not used.

ENCOURAGING WILDLIFE

Some trees have features that are particularly attractive to wildlife. Densely leaved trees, such as the evergreen conifers *Chamaecyparis*, *Cupressus*, and *Thuja*, provide ideal shelter and cover for birds, especially in cold winters. Hawthorns (*Crataegus*) are also good, in particular the forms of *C. laevigata* or *C. monogyna*.

There is usually plenty of food available for nectar-feeding insects, such as pollinating bees, butterflies, or moths, at the peak of the flowering season. For most trees, this is in mid- to late spring, so it is useful to include some trees that flower either earlier or later. *Amelanchier*, for example, flowers early in the year; it also produces fruits early, providing food for birds in summer, when berries are otherwise scarce. Late-flowering trees that are good for wildlife include *Buddleja alternifolia* and *Stewartia pseudocamellia*. Both flower in summer.

> ### Encourage songbirds to the garden: they will help keep many pests at bay

Any of the berrying trees are a valuable source of food in autumn and winter, with hawthorns, hollies, and whitebeams and rowans (*Sorbus*) among the best. If you are choosing a hawthorn with the purpose of attracting wildlife, avoid those with double flowers, since they do not produce fruit. Hollies (*Ilex*) are excellent, since their fruits are persistent, providing food well into winter. Yellow fruits are less attractive to birds, so choose trees with red fruits.

To attract a wider range of wildlife, consider developing "wild" or moist areas, such as a pond or boggy area, within the garden. Plant shrubs and perennials, as well as trees, to provide food and shelter and to encourage birds and other animals.

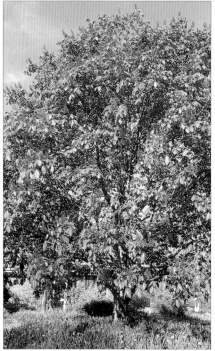

ATTRACTION FOR BEES
The eye-catching, tubular red flowers of Aesculus pavia *attract a variety of bees and other insects in late spring and early summer.*

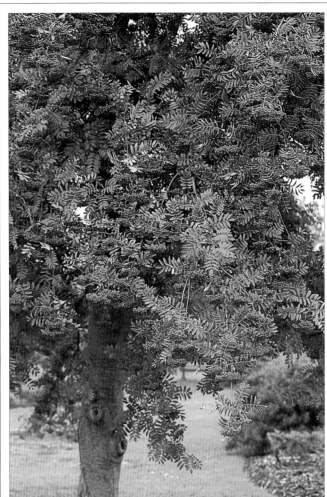

◄ FEAST FOR BIRDS
*The striking orange-
red fruits of the
rowan* (Sorbus
aucuparia) *are very
attractive to birds
when they ripen,
providing welcome
food in autumn.*

▼ REFUGE FOR BIRDS
*Fruits tempt birds to
feed in a garden in
autumn, while a
carefully positioned
nesting box will
encourage them to
become permanent
residents.*

FAVOURITES FOR WILDLIFE

Aesculus (bees, butterflies, and birds)
Amelanchier (bees, butterflies, and birds)
Caragana (bees, butterflies, and birds)
Chamaecyparis (roosting sites for birds)
Crataegus (bees, butterflies, and birds)
Cupressus (roosting sites for birds)
Ilex (bees, butterflies, and birds)
Malus (bees, butterflies, and birds)
Sorbus (bees, butterflies, and birds)
Stewartia (bees, butterflies, and birds)
Thuja (roosting sites for birds)

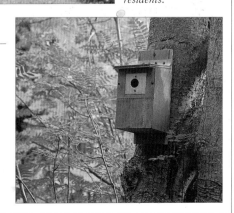

CONTAINER TREES

CONTAINERS BRING A GREAT degree of flexibility to planting, and are ideal for small gardens where planting space may be limited or even non-existent, such as on a roof or in a basement courtyard. A great advantage of containers is that they are easy to move around, enabling ever-changing displays. They also allow you to grow trees that have specific needs, such as tender trees, which can be moved to a protected place for winter, or trees that require an acid soil.

CHOOSING AND PLACING TREES

Many trees are suitable for growing in containers. The best are those that are naturally small or slow-growing, or ones that may be pruned regularly. Large, fast-growing trees, such as birches (*Betula*), soon outgrow their containers and may become top-heavy and subject to blowing over in strong winds.

For long-term display, choose an evergreen such as *Pittosporum tenuifolium* or the yew *Taxus baccata* 'Standishii', or a deciduous tree grown for its foliage, such as *Acer palmatum*, particularly the cut-leaved forms. If there is space for a range of trees, you could consider those with effects over a shorter period, such as flowering trees, including *Hydrangea paniculata* and *Caragana arborescens* trained as standards, or some of the flowering cherries: *Prunus* 'Amanogawa' would be a good choice.

Trees in containers associate well with formal plantings, and are particularly suited to the areas close to the house. They

For roof gardens, choose lightweight containers, such as plastic or wood

are useful for extending the garden onto paved areas, for example a patio, or may be used to highlight certain areas or structures, such as a gateway, flight of steps, or a door. Potted trees combine well with other container-grown plants, including shrubs, perennials, and annuals, to provide an exciting range of effects. For variety (and providing they are not too

GROUPING CONTAINERS
Container trees have real impact when combined with other plants, their height adding interest to any display. Here, the silvery foliage of Elaeagnus angustifolia *contrasts with a range of colourful perennials.*

SUNNY SITES
Caragana arborescens 'Pendula'
Cordyline australis
Eriobotrya japonica
Ficus carica
Hydrangea paniculata
Lagerstroemia
Laurus nobilis
Ligustrum lucidum
Pinus sylvestris 'Fastigiata'
Prunus 'Amanogawa',
P. 'Kiku-shidare-zakura'

SHADY SITES
Acer palmatum
Ilex
Laurus nobilis
Ligustrum lucidum
Photinia × *fraseri*
Pittosporum tenuifolium
Taxus baccata 'Fastigiata'
and 'Standishii'

EVERGREEN DISPLAY
Placed in a prominent position and pruned to retain a compact shape (see p.56), *Ilex* × *altaclerensis* '*Golden King*' *makes an attractive year-round feature.*

heavy), move the containers around to create changing combinations of flowering or foliage plants. Place container trees that flower or fruit briefly but profusely in a prominent location when they are at their best, to make the most of their assets. After the period of interest is over, move them to another, less conspicuous position in the garden, perhaps in a border.

CHOOSING CONTAINERS
There is a wide range of different pots available, made from a variety of materials including wood, stone, terracotta, plastic, and fibreglass. Stone and terracotta pots are attractive but relatively heavy, so if

weight is a consideration, for example on a roof-top, choose lightweight containers, such as those made of plastic, fibreglass, or wood. Since trees are long-lived, it is important to select a container that will last. While wooden or plastic containers are relatively inexpensive, they tend to rot or split. Unless the garden is very mild, choose a pot that is frost-proof, since some containers (particularly terracotta) can be damaged by very cold weather.

Always consider which size, colour, and shape of pot will suit the tree as well as the style and scale of the garden. A container should add to rather than detract from the area in which it is placed.

PATIO FEATURE
*The many forms
of* Acer palmatum
*make delightful
foliage plants, and
adapt extremely well
to containers. They
require a sheltered
site, preferably with
some shade from very
hot sun, and may
need some protection
from late frosts.*

TOWN GARDENS

Gardens in towns or cities may be very small, often mostly paved, and with little area for planting. They are therefore ideal sites for using trees in containers. Such gardens are also likely to be subject to special climatic conditions. They may well be relatively mild and sheltered from wind, and can be very shady but with some parts exposed to periods of hot sun. Trees therefore need to be chosen accordingly. If conditions are particularly mild, a town garden can provide the opportunity to experiment with some trees normally grown in subtropical areas, such as citrus fruits or palms.

In a very small garden, choose mainly evergreen trees, or deciduous ones with attractive foliage to ensure a long season of interest. Aim to keep the size of the tree to scale with the garden. Container trees will form only part of the ornamental attractions, so allow sufficient space for other pots of flowering shrubs, perennials, and annuals to create a display that is effective all year. In cities, where the air may be polluted, select trees that will tolerate these conditions, such as bay laurel (*Laurus nobilis*) and yews (*Taxus*). For very exposed, windy roof-tops, avoid trees that may become top-heavy, such as cordylines.

TREES FOR TOWNS

Acer japonicum, A. palmatum
Cordyline australis
Cupressus sempervirens
Eriobotrya japonica
Ficus carica
Ilex × *altaclerensis, I. aquifolium*
Lagerstroemia indica
Laurus nobilis
Ligustrum lucidum 'Excelsum Superbum'
Photinia × *fraseri*
Pittosporum tenuifolium
Taxus baccata 'Fastigiata' and 'Standishii'

CARING FOR TREES IN POTS

Trees grown in containers need more careful maintenance than those planted in the open ground. Since the small quantity of compost in a pot can hold only limited amounts of water and nutrients, trees in containers can dry out easily, and will eventually become depleted of nutrients. At planting, use a good, loam-based compost with an added slow-release fertilizer. During hot weather, you may need to water twice a day (if the tree dislikes lime, and your water is hard, use only rain water collected in a butt). The compost should always remain slightly moist. To prevent drying out, apply bark chippings, cocoa shells, or pebbles to the compost surface. Waterlogging is also often a problem for container plants, so always incorporate a layer of broken crocks or coarse gravel at the base of the container before planting.

Every year, in spring, remove the mulch and the top 5cm (2in) of compost, then replace it with fresh compost with added fertilizer. Every three to five years, again in spring, repot the tree into either the same or a larger container. To repot, remove the

Container trees need frequent watering and repotting every few years

tree from its container, tease out the roots, and remove some of the old compost, cutting back any large, thick roots by up to one-third. Soak the root ball if necessary, and repot the tree using fresh compost and mulch. Prune container trees in the same way as you would trees grown in the open ground (*see pp.50–53*).

◄ TOWN GARDEN
An array of container plants, including the evergreen trees Cordyline australis *and* Pittosporum tenuifolium, *create an attractive display in this courtyard garden.*

▼ BLUE SPRUCE
Conifers like this Picea pungens *f.* glauca *are good container trees, since their roots do not require much space.*

TREES WITH OTHER PLANTS

WHILE TREES CAN LOOK SPLENDID in an isolated position, for example when planted at the end of a vista, they can also be grown very effectively with other plants, including bulbs, herbaceous perennials, shrubs, and climbers. Depending on the look you wish to achieve, you can either combine plants that flower or fruit at the same time as the tree, in contrasting or complementary colours, or extend the season by providing interest at other times of the year.

WHAT KIND OF TREE?

When growing trees in combination with other plants, one of the main points to consider is the amount of shade that the tree produces, since this will determine which plants may be grown beneath. Birches, for example, cast relatively little shade, but they are hungry feeders and quickly remove water and nutrients from the soil. Heathers (*Calluna*, *Erica*), brooms (*Cytisus*), and *Cistus* are therefore ideal planting companions, since they thrive in a light position and a poor soil. Beneath trees that create denser shade, for example many spreading or weeping trees, you will need to choose plants that require little light.

Bulbous plants that produce their flowers and foliage before the tree's leaves are fully open are excellent under trees.

The shape and size of the tree are also important factors. A strongly pendulous tree with branches weeping to the ground will hide anything planted beneath it, except perhaps for some early-flowering bulbs. An upright tree, however, will be able to accommodate a broader selection of plants at its base.

LIGHT, AIRY CANOPY
The light shade cast by Betula utilis *var.* jacquemontii *allows a wide range of plants to grow beneath, providing an ample foil to its handsome white bark.*

▲ SPRING DISPLAY
Prunus pendula *creates dense shade in summer, but the grape hyacinths and primroses bloom before the leaves are fully open.*

► USEFUL PARTNERS
Clematis alpina *is an ideal climber for a small tree. Plant it at the canopy edge and train it using a cane.*

SHADE-LOVING PLANTS TO GROW WITH TREES

BULBS
Anemone
Cyclamen
Eranthis
Galanthus
Hyacinthoides
Erythronium
Scilla
Trillium

PERENNIALS
Anemone (Japanese anemones)
Astilbe
Astrantia
Bergenia
Digitalis
Epimedium
Euphorbia amygdaloides subsp. *robbiae*
Hosta

CLIMBERS
Actinidia kolomikta
Clematis (some)
Eccremocarpus scaber
Humulus lupulus 'Aureus'
Lathyrus latifolius
Lonicera
Rosa
Tropaeolum speciosum

SHRUBS
Aucuba japonica
Daphne laureola
Euonymus (evergreen sorts)
Fatsia japonica
Mahonia
Pieris
Skimmia
Vinca

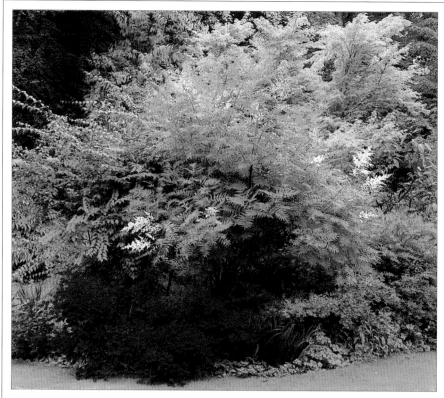

▲ SHRUBBY SCHEME
A young maple, Acer palmatum *'Senkaki', combines with shrubs including* Sorbaria aitchisonii *and* Rosa nitida *in an island bed to create a blend of texture and colour.*

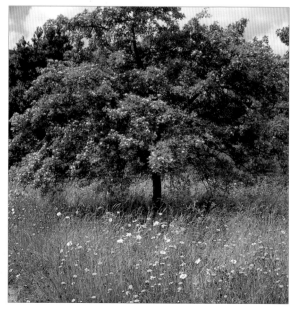

▶ NATURAL SETTING
Areas of the garden intended to have a natural appearance, such as a wildflower planting, are best complemented by trees that blend in well with the landscape, for example this Crataegus laciniata.

USING TREES WITH OTHER PLANTS

If a tree is intended as a specimen, then avoid underplanting with large shrubs, since they will mask the trunk and shape of the tree. Instead, choose low, spreading plants, such as periwinkles (*Vinca*) or creeping junipers (*Juniperus horizontalis*), both of which will accentuate a tree's form. However, if the tree is used for screening, you could use larger plants, such as *Prunus laurocerasus* and *Viburnum tinus*, which will help to fill in the screen.

> Many early-flowering
> bulbs grow happily
> under densely shady trees

Trees also add substance to mixed borders. When selecting plants to associate with trees, consider which ones are in flower when the tree is at its best for maximum impact. Alternatively, use other plants to provide interest over a long period, and to enliven the border when the tree is not in its prime. Where a few small trees are grown together, the area can soon begin to take on a "woodland" feel, particularly if underplanted with herbaceous perennials such as astrantias, epimediums, and hostas.

Trees are the perfect hosts for many climbing plants: the trunk and branches provide essential support, while the climber adorns the tree with its additional crop of flowers. The climber must be compatible with the tree. For small ornamental trees, avoid very vigorous climbers, such as wisteria and *Clematis montana*, and instead use slower-growing species such as C. *alpina* and C. *macropetala*.

Ivies are commonly grown as ground cover under trees, and most will grow well in shade. For best effect, use the more vigorous ones, such as *Hedera colchica* 'Dentata Variegata' and *H. hibernica*, in the shadiest places. Climbing ivies may eventually smother a small, ornamental tree, so cut them back before they become a problem. Allow ivies to establish and climb naturally if desired, rather than training them with a support.

LAWN HIGHLIGHTS
Trees are best planted slightly to the side of a lawn, not in the centre. Removing the lower branches makes the grass easier to cut and maintain (see pp.52–53, 55).

TREES FOR LAWNS

Catalpa bignoniodes 'Aurea'
Cercis siliquastrum
Fagus sylvatica 'Dawyck Gold'
Genista aetnensis
Koelreuteria paniculata
Magnolia obovata
Malus (many)
Prunus (many)
Sorbus (many)
Trachycarpus fortunei

PLANTING AND TREE CARE

SELECTING A TREE

ANY GARDEN TREE IS A LONG-TERM investment, so it is worth taking some time to decide which tree to plant and where, and to select a good and healthy specimen. This could mean the difference between a plant that grows away quickly, or one that produces little or no growth. If possible, buy the tree from the garden centre or nursery where it has been grown. Always check that any tree you choose is suited to the conditions that your garden provides.

ESTABLISHING YOUR TREES

Once you have selected a suitable tree for the site, it is vital to give it proper attention before, during, and after planting. Prepare the planting hole thoroughly, and always plant the tree at the correct height, never too deeply, since it may sink even lower as the soil settles. After planting, water well, and then frequently for the first year. Check tree ties regularly: overly tight ties can damage and eventually kill a tree. Also, look out for any signs of pests and diseases (*see pp.58–59*) and animal damage (*see p.48*). Any vegetation around the tree's base will compete for water and nutrients, so keep the area free of weeds and grass.

TIPS FOR SUCCESS
• Ensure that the ultimate size of your chosen tree is suitable for the position in which you wish to plant it.
• Select a healthy, well-shaped specimen.
• Never allow the tree roots to dry out, either before or after planting.
• Check for signs of pests and diseases, and remedy promptly.

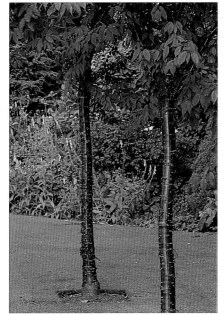

ORNAMENTAL BARK
When choosing a tree for bark, such as these Prunus serrula, *examine them before buying to ensure they have clean, undamaged stems.*

◄ ADAPTABLE CHOICE Acer pseudoplatanus '*Brilliantissimum*' *thrives in sun or partial shade.*

ASSESSING THE SOIL

A HEALTHY SOIL IS VITAL for trees to thrive. The ideal soil contains a well-balanced mixture of clay and sand; it will drain freely but retain moisture, and is high in nutrients. Too much clay can result in a heavy soil that may become waterlogged when wet. A sandy soil may be impoverished and dry out fast. The type of soil in your garden – whether it is acid or alkaline, or has a high clay or sand content – will determine which trees you can best grow, so it is essential to assess it thoroughly before you decide which tree to plant.

TESTING YOUR SOIL pH

Most trees thrive in a slightly acid soil, but some do not tolerate alkalinity, particularly if the soil is dry and shallow. The effects of lime include yellowing leaves, little growth, and poor autumn colour. The pH of a soil – its level of acidity or alkalinity – is alterable to some extent, but not usually successfully for trees, owing to their wide-spreading roots. If you have alkaline soil, it is best not to grow acid-loving trees, such as most eucryphias and some magnolias. Instead, choose those that tolerate lime, such as laburnums or flowering cherries.

A yellow or orange colour indicates acid soil

Bright green indicates neutral soil

Dark green indicates alkaline soil

USING A SOIL-TESTING KIT
Do-it-yourself kits are an effective way to measure your soil pH. For the result, simply match the colour in the tube against a chart.

SOIL TEXTURE

The best garden soil is a loam, with a good, crumbly texture, not too sticky or gritty when moist, and with ample organic matter. A good soil retains moisture so that it does not dry out easily, and drains freely so that it does not become waterlogged. Soils that have a high clay content tend to be fertile but poorly drained and heavy; sandy soils are easier to work but are low in nutrients and subject to drying out; silty soils become easily compacted.

Moist and heavy; can be squeezed into shape

Dry and gritty in texture

CLAY SOIL
Highly moisture-retentive, a clay soil is sticky and smooth.

SANDY SOIL
A sandy soil drains very freely, so tends to be light and dry.

SOIL TIPS

• Nearby gardens usually provide a good guide to a soil's pH. If rhododendrons and camellias thrive, then your soil is almost certainly acidic.

• Test more than one area of the garden. Some areas, such as at the foot of a wall, may contain more lime than others.

• Several trees are suited to heavy clay soils, such as some maples (*Acer negundo*, *A. pseudoplatanus*), horse chestnuts (*Aesculus*), hawthorns (*Crataegus*), and hollies (*Ilex*).

• Trees that grow well on light, sandy soils include birches (*Betula*), *Caragana*, *Cercis*, *Koelreuteria*, and *Robinia*.

IMPROVING THE SOIL

You can improve the texture, drainage, moisture retention, and fertility of soil considerably by digging in a soil improver. If you have a clay soil, coarse horticultural sand combined with organic matter or lime will increase aeration and drainage. For sandy soils, add organic matter and small amounts of clay, which will increase water retention and essential nutrients. Silty soils benefit from adding organic matter and a small amount of clay or lime to improve the structure and prevent compaction.

Manure supplies organic matter and nutrients

Coarse sand improves drainage of heavy soils

Chipped bark improves water retention and adds nutrients

Leaf mould encourages earthworms and adds nutrients

SOIL IMPROVERS

• Composted manure (especially horse manure) and leaf mould add nutrients to the soil, increase water retention, and encourage earthworms, which aerate the soil.
• Coarse sand will improve drainage in clay soils (always use horticultural sand, never builder's materials). Large amounts may be needed if the soil is very heavy.
• Small amounts of clay added to a sandy or silty soil will improve the soil structure, increase water retention, and add nutrients.
• Lime is useful for improving the structure of heavy or compacted soils. Never use lime at the same time as manure, and avoid it if you grow trees that require an acid soil.
• Mulches, such as leaf mould and chipped bark, keep moisture in the soil, reduce weeds, and protect roots from frost. Apply them to the soil surface but do not dig them in.

PREPARING THE SOIL FOR PLANTING

Before undertaking any planting, it is essential to prepare the site thoroughly. If planting in spring, begin preparations in autumn, especially in heavy soils, since any large lumps will be broken down by winter frosts. Remove perennial weeds, especially the more vigorous ones such as couch grass, ground elder, and bindweed. If the area is overgrown, cut down the vegetation first, then dig out the roots. Even with the most rigorous methods of cultivation, some small pieces of root will remain. Remove them as the plants appear, before they can become established. Alternatively, use a translocated weedkiller, which moves within the plant from the leaves to the roots. Once the area is cleared of weeds, dig in plenty of organic matter.

DIGGING IN
To improve moisture retention and increase the nutrient content of the soil, dig in ample quantities of organic matter, such as leaf mould, manure, or well-rotted compost.

BUYING TREES

A WIDE RANGE OF POPULAR trees is usually available at garden centres; however, if you are looking for something a little more unusual, you may need to visit a specialist nursery. Alternatively, some nurseries run a mail-order service. Trees are sold bare-root, root-balled, or in containers, depending on the type of tree and time of year. All trees, particularly bare-root and root-balled trees, are best planted as soon as possible after purchasing.

WHAT TO LOOK FOR

Before buying a tree, ensure that it is suitable for the site and is a healthy, well-shaped specimen. Inspect the shoots and, if the tree is in foliage, the leaves, since both indicate the health of the plant. The main stem must be straight and intact, and there should be a single, well-formed leader (one main shoot that is growing vertically).

CRATAEGUS LAEVIGATA
'PAUL'S SCARLET'

CRATAEGUS LAEVIGATA
'PAUL'S SCARLET'
• **Season of interest:** Late spring to early summer.
• **Height:** 8m (25ft)
• **Spread:** 8m (25ft)
• **Hardiness:** Fully hardy
• **Soil type:** Any that is not waterlogged. Suitable for clay and chalk soil.
• **Aspect:** Sun or partial shade. Suitable for exposed positions.

BUYING HINTS
• Small trees are not only less expensive than larger ones, but are also easier to plant, quicker to establish, and require less aftercare.
• Check that the eventual size of the tree will not be too large for your garden.
• Buy stakes and ties when you purchase your tree.

◄ CHECK THE PLANT LABEL
The label gives vital details of the tree's appearance, size after five or ten years, and cultivation requirements.

BARE-ROOT TREES

Trees that are sold bare-root are usually deciduous, and are available only during the dormant season (between autumn and early spring). They are grown in the open ground and lifted with little or no soil, so the root system is very susceptible to drying out. Check that the roots are healthy, evenly spread, and have not dried out. Leave the wrapping on for protection until the tree is planted. If you cannot plant the tree straight away, keep the roots moist and protected from drying winds by heeling in (*see Planting Tips, p.47*).

Evenly spreading roots

Coiled, congested roots

GOOD EXAMPLE
Well-developed roots that are spread in all directions are the sign of a healthy tree.

POOR EXAMPLE
Avoid trees with congested or coiled roots: they will rarely establish successfully.

ROOT-BALLED TREES

As with bare-root trees, root-balled ones are grown in the open ground, but are lifted with a ball of soil around their roots. A hessian or similar wrapping holds the root ball together and prevents drying out. Both deciduous and evergreen trees may be sold this way. The advantage of a root-balled tree is that there is less damage to the root system, and it is likely to retain moisture better than a bare-root tree. Like bare-root trees, root-balled trees are normally available only between autumn and early spring. Before buying, check that the root ball is firm, intact, and has not dried out. If the tree cannot be planted immediately, keep the root ball moist by watering and, if the tree is evergreen, protect it from drying winds.

HEALTHY ROOT-BALLED TREE
Many evergreen trees, particularly conifers, are often available for purchase as root-balled specimens.

Top growth should appear healthy

The root ball should be firm and the hessian intact

CONTAINER-GROWN TREES

Available throughout the year, container-grown trees are evergreen or deciduous, and may be planted at any time. Before buying, gently remove the tree from its container, if possible, and inspect the root system. If you see a mass of roots circling the pot, or emerging from its base, then the tree is "pot bound" and best avoided. Keep the compost moist, and the tree in a sheltered site until planting.

◀ GOOD EXAMPLE
This is a healthy container-grown tree with the best chance of survival: some roots are visible and the root ball is firm.

▼ POOR EXAMPLE
The dense mass of congested roots and liverworts on the compost surface indicate a pot-bound tree that is unlikely to establish well.

Root ball is often small in relation to top growth

Evenly spaced branch framework

Mesh may restrict growth

TREE ROOTS IN MESH
Some mature trees are sold with their roots in mesh within a container. Cut the mesh and soak the root ball before planting.

Healthy, well-developed roots

Liverworts on compost

Compost free of liverworts, weeds, and algae

Pot-bound root system

PLANTING A TREE

CAREFUL ATTENTION to site preparation and planting greatly increases a tree's ability to establish and grow strongly, rendering it more resistant to disease. Adding well-rotted organic matter will give the tree an excellent start. If planting in spring, add about 110g (4oz) of slow-release fertilizer. For the first two or three years after planting, provide plenty of water, keep the area below the tree weed free, and feed and mulch regularly, not allowing the mulch to touch the trunk. It is easier to plant the tree with a helper to hold it vertical.

HOW TO PLANT A CONTAINER-GROWN TREE

The compost in a container can dry out very quickly, particularly in warm weather and when a tree is in leaf. Once dry, it can be very difficult to wet again after planting.

To prevent a tree from drying out, place the container in water for 30 minutes before planting. Take the tree out of the container only when you are ready to plant.

1 **Mark out** a circular hole, 3–4 times the diameter of the pot. Remove any turf and weeds from the surface, and dig the hole to 1½ times the depth of the pot.

2 **Using a fork**, break up the soil at the sides and base of the hole to enable roots to penetrate more easily. Mix any removed soil with well-rotted organic matter.

3 **Lay the tree** on its side and carefully slide it out of the container. Gently tease out the outer roots without damaging the root ball. This will help the tree to establish.

4 **Insert the stake firmly**, slightly off-centre, towards the direction of the wind. Add about one-fifth of the mixed soil and organic matter to the hole. Place the tree. Use a cane to check that the top of the root ball is level with the soil.

5 **Backfill with** the rest of the soil and organic matter, firming evenly by treading. Tie the tree to the stake. Water and mulch. Cut back any damaged shoots.

How to Plant a Root-balled Tree

Root-balled trees have a stronger root system and are usually easier to establish than container-grown trees, since they are grown in soil in the open ground rather than in compost in a container. However, the disadvantage is that some of the roots are invariably damaged on lifting and, if the root ball breaks up, further damage is possible. Many evergreen trees, such as conifers, are grown in this way.

PLANTING TIPS

• Plant root-balled trees as soon as possible after buying, from autumn to early spring.
• Take great care when handling root-balled trees. Aim to keep the root ball intact.
• If dry, water gently before planting, but never immerse in water.
• Shelter newly planted evergreens with windbreaks made from canes and netting.

1 **Prepare the planting hole** as for container-grown trees (*see facing page*), but make the hole 2–3 times the diameter of the root ball. Place the tree in the hole and loosen the wrapping.

2 **Carefully remove** the wrapping by tilting the tree first to one side, then the other. Insert the stake or stakes now, if necessary. Backfill with the removed soil and organic matter. Firm, water, and mulch.

How to Plant a Bare-root Tree

The advantage of bare-root trees is that they can be lifted with a considerable network of strong roots. Plant them as for container-grown trees (*see facing page*), but make the hole just wide enough to take the roots when spread out. Cut off any damaged roots before planting. Drive in a stake, then make a small mound of loose soil in the centre of the hole. Place the tree on the mound and spread out the roots.

PLANTING TIPS

• Plant as soon as possible after purchase, between autumn and early spring.
• Retain the covering around the roots until planting.
• If you can't plant the tree immediately, heel it in by covering the roots with moist soil in a trench until you are ready to plant.

1 **Using a cane,** line up the soil mark on the stem so that it is flush with the level of the surrounding soil.

2 **Gently firm** the soil to ensure that no large spaces are left around the roots. Water and mulch.

How to Stake and Tie a Tree

Until the root systems are established, all but the smallest trees benefit from staking. The best stake is very sturdy, and allows the head of the tree to move but keeps the base firm. In most cases, a low single stake is preferable. In windy sites, use a low angled stake or two stakes. High single stakes are needed only for trees with well-branched heads and a slender stem, such as crab apples (*Malus*); cut the stake down to a short stake after the first year. For strong support, use guy ropes (*see facing page*).

LOW STAKE
Use a low stake set vertically. For container-grown trees, set the stake at an angle of 45° leaning into the wind.

TWO STAKES
In windy conditions, use two vertical stakes, one on either side of the root ball (ideal for container-grown trees).

STAKING TIPS

• Place a protective wooden block on the stake before driving it in to prevent the stake from splitting.
• Drive in the stake or stakes before planting, at about 60cm (24in) below soil level (*see p.46*).
• Ensure the stake does not rub against the tree's stem.
• Remove stakes after two to three years.
• Always use proprietary ties to secure a tree to a stake, as shown below.

◄ BUCKLE AND SPACER TIE
This tie prevents the stake from rubbing against the tree, and is adjustable to allow for growth. Tie it so that it is taut but will not damage the bark.

◄ RUBBER TIE
If you use a rubber tree tie without a buckle, nail it very firmly to the stake to prevent it from slipping and causing damage to the bark by friction.

Protecting the Stem

Deer, rabbits, and even scratching cats can cause irreversible harm to the bark of a young tree. If the damage is severe, the tree is likely to die. In some areas, it is vital to provide some form of protection for young trees. Spiral tree guards, made of flexible plastic that wraps around the stem, provide excellent protection, as do many other proprietary guards available. Wire mesh, supported by stakes, is also highly effective. A barrier of netting that extends well below ground level will deter burrowing rabbits; insert it well clear of the roots.

SPIRAL STEM GUARD   WIRE MESH

TRANSPLANTING A YOUNG TREE

If you wish to move a tree, it is best to transplant it when it is small, up to about 2.5m (8ft) tall. Small trees are not only easier to move, but are also quicker to establish in their new position. Larger trees may require professional attention.

Prepare the ground one year in advance of the planned move. In early autumn, mark out a circle around the tree with a diameter about one-third of the height of the tree. Outside the marked area, dig a trench 30cm (12in) wide and 60cm (24in) deep. Cut through any roots cleanly with a sharp spade and undercut the tree as far as possible. Refill the trench with the soil mixed with organic matter.

1 **In autumn** the following year, dig another trench just outside the previous one to the same width and depth. Carefully fork away the soil from around the root ball.

2 **Taking care not** to damage the roots, undercut the root ball with a spade and, using secateurs, cut back any awkward roots protruding from the root ball.

3 **Lay a length** of hessian or plastic sheet beside the tree. Tilting the tree first to one side and then the other, slide the sheet underneath the root ball.

4 **Bring up the sides** of the sheet around the root ball. Tie it securely in place with ropes that pass around and underneath the root ball to keep it intact in the move.

5 **Move the tree** to its new site, lowering it into a pre-dug planting hole (see p.46) using the ropes. Remove the sheet, then replant the tree to the soil mark on the stem.

6 **When the tree** has been replanted, secure the tree with angled stakes and guy ropes. Water well and cover the ground around it with a 10cm (4in) layer of mulch.

PRUNING BASICS

Y OUNG TREES, ESPECIALLY those that are deciduous, benefit from correct pruning and training to ensure the development of a well-shaped and balanced head. Mature trees, unless they are coppiced or pollarded (*see p.57*), usually require little pruning, although they may need to have the occasional wayward or crossing branches removed, or dead or diseased wood cut out.

CHOOSING THE RIGHT TOOL FOR THE JOB

Whichever job you are undertaking, selecting the appropriate tool makes the task easier, safer, and yields better results. The tool you use will depend on the size of the stem or branch that you intend to cut.

Invest in good-quality tools, and look after them properly. Keeping them clean and sharp is vital: a clean cut heals more quickly and is less liable to become infected.

Sharp cutting blade

Safety catch

Bright handles make them easy to find

Buffers prevent jarring when cutting

SECATEURS
Use secateurs to cut woody shoots up to approximately 1cm (½in) thick, or for taking cuttings.

LOPPERS
For thick woody shoots 1–2.5cm (½–1in) thick, and for inaccessible stems, loppers are just right.

GARDEN KNIFE
A sharp, folding knife is useful for several tasks, such as light pruning, and for taking cuttings.

PRUNING SAW
Good for general-purpose pruning, this short-bladed saw can be used even in confined spaces.

LOOKING AFTER YOUR TOOLS
• Store tools in a dry place.
• After use, clean cutting blades by wiping over with an oily rag or steel wool, dry well, then oil lightly.
• Keep blades sharp (saw blades should be sharpened by a professional).
• Replace any damaged blades when necessary.

DOUBLE-EDGED PRUNING SAW
This flexible saw has both coarse- and fine-toothed sides.

Clamp holds blade taut

BOW SAW
Ideal for cutting thick branches or even the trunk of a small tree.

How to Use Your Tools

Careful and correct use of pruning tools is vital for your safety and the health of the tree. Using tools incorrectly can result in poor cuts that damage the plant and may lead to infection and disease. The correct use of secateurs, loppers, and a garden knife is shown below. For how to use a bow saw and pruning saw, see page 55.

SECATEURS
Use secateurs with the thin cutting blade as close to the stem junction or bud as possible for a close cut.

LOPPERS
When using loppers, attempt to cut only shoots that will fit comfortably between the two blades.

GARDEN KNIFE
Smooth the rough edges of pruning cuts with a garden knife. This is essential to prevent infection.

COMMON MISTAKES

Pruning incorrectly, by using a tool in the wrong way, or by using one that is not suitable for the job, can damage both the plant and the tool. A common mistake is to try to use a single tool, such as secateurs, for all pruning work, regardless of scale. Always use the right tool for the job, and never use the tool for any other purpose, such as cutting pieces of wire or lengths of string.

Thick blade is nearer the trunk, leaving a stub

INCORRECT USE
Cutting with secateurs held the wrong way around, as here, can leave a stub that is liable to die back.

Damaged tissue

INCORRECT TOOL
This shoot is too thick to cut with secateurs. Twisting them will damage both the plant and the secateurs.

When and Where to Prune

The best time to prune most deciduous trees is in late autumn or winter. Other times are possible for most trees, except for maples (*Acer*), chestnuts (*Aesculus*), birches (*Betula*), and cherries (*Prunus*). Avoid pruning these in late winter or early spring, since they bleed sap when cut then. Prune all stems to just above a healthy bud: cutting too far above leaves a length of shoot that will die back, while cutting too close may damage the bud. The angle of cut depends on the position of the buds.

Straight cut

OPPOSITE BUDS
Where the buds are opposite, make a straight cut just above a pair of buds.

Angled cut

ALTERNATE BUDS
Where the buds are alternate, make an angled cut above a strong bud.

TRAINING YOUNG TREES

DECIDUOUS TREES are often sold ready-trained as "standards", with a clear stem and branched head. However, you can also buy them in "feathered" form, with side branches often to ground level, and train them yourself. This is both less expensive and more effective, since younger trees are quicker to establish than mature ones. The tree type will determine the training method.

FORMING A STANDARD TREE

The aim of this method, suitable for birches (*Betula*) for example, is to have a clear length of stem at the base by retaining the strong-growing central or leading shoot and removing the lower branches over two to three years.

On upper third of main stem, cut back only poor growth and badly placed or crossing shoots

Shorten side shoots in middle by two-thirds

On upper third, remove badly placed or crossing shoots

On middle third, shorten side shoots by half

Check and loosen tie if necessary

On upper third, remove badly placed or crossing shoots

Remove all side shoots on lowest third

Remove lowest side shoots

Cut back all lower side shoots on the desired length of clear stem

As the crown of branches develops, remove any crossing shoots

YEAR 1, WINTER   YEARS 2 AND 3, WINTER   YEAR 4, WINTER

TRAINING A LEADING SHOOT

A single, straight leading shoot is essential if you are training a tree as a standard. If a competing leading shoot develops, remove it as soon as possible by cutting it off at the base. Where two or more leading shoots have been allowed to develop, select the strongest and straightest and remove its weaker competitor(s) (*see right*).

To replace a broken or damaged leading shoot, attach a cane to the main stem, and tie in another strong shoot (*see far right*). Prune back the broken shoot to the base.

SELECTING A LEADER   REPLACING A LEADER

FORMING A ROUND-HEADED TREE

For the first two or three years, train as for a standard tree (*see facing page*), then cut out the leading shoot. Suitable for most hawthorns (*Crataegus*), crab apples (*Malus*), and cherries (*Prunus*), this method will cause the tree to branch and spread horizontally.

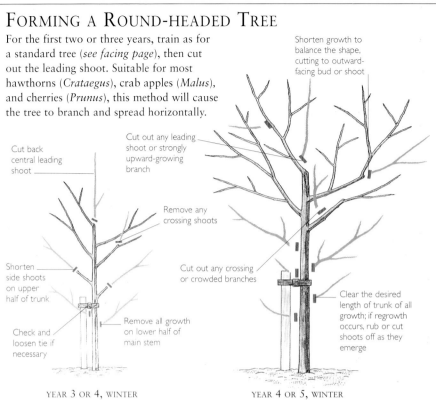

Shorten growth to balance the shape, cutting to outward-facing bud or shoot

Cut out any leading shoot or strongly upward-growing branch

Cut back central leading shoot

Remove any crossing shoots

Shorten side shoots on upper half of trunk

Cut out any crossing or crowded branches

Check and loosen tie if necessary

Remove all growth on lower half of main stem

Clear the desired length of trunk of all growth; if regrowth occurs, rub or cut shoots off as they emerge

YEAR 3 OR 4, WINTER

YEAR 4 OR 5, WINTER

FORMING A FEATHERED TREE

While many feathered trees are best trained into standards or round-headed trees, others require little pruning and are more attractive when allowed to branch from the base to retain the feathered shape. Various upright forms of hornbeams (*Carpinus*), beeches (*Fagus*), and many evergreens are grown in this way.

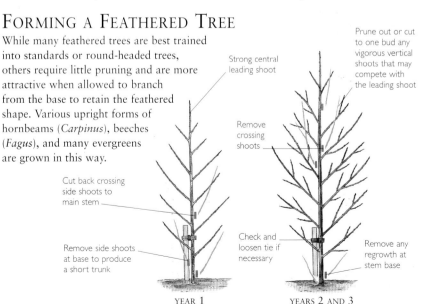

Strong central leading shoot

Prune out or cut to one bud any vigorous vertical shoots that may compete with the leading shoot

Remove crossing shoots

Cut back crossing side shoots to main stem

Remove side shoots at base to produce a short trunk

Check and loosen tie if necessary

Remove any regrowth at stem base

YEAR 1

YEARS 2 AND 3

PRUNING MATURE TREES

GENERALLY, MATURE TREES require little pruning. However, when a tree becomes damaged or diseased, or causes an obstruction, action is needed. If a branch breaks, cut it back to an outward-facing bud on the same shoot or to its base. Cut diseased shoots back to a bud on healthy wood, which will show no discoloration when cut. If, after pruning, a shoot forms from a lower bud, leaving a stub of dead wood, cut this back to just above the new shoot.

REMOVING SUCKERS AND WATER SHOOTS

Many trees produce suckers, which are shoots that arise from the roots or the base of the trunk. These quickly become unsightly and take nutrients from the tree. Depending on their size, rub them off or cut them back to the base. More new suckers may be produced, which should be rubbed off as they appear. Water shoots are unwanted, vigorous shoots that arise from the trunk or branches after pruning. Cut them back to the base with secateurs.

SUCKERS
Cut suckers off where they arise, and rub off any new ones that may appear.

WATER SHOOTS
Water shoots may arise from pruning wounds. Cut them off at the base.

CORRECTING UNEVEN GROWTH

If a small tree has grown to produce an unevenly shaped head, you can correct this by pruning. Prune the strong side lightly, and the weak side more heavily to stimulate growth of strong new shoots.

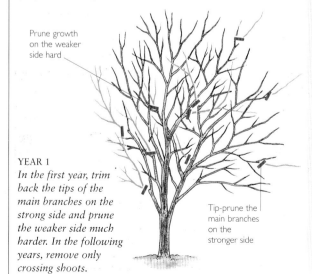

Prune growth on the weaker side hard

YEAR 1
In the first year, trim back the tips of the main branches on the strong side and prune the weaker side much harder. In the following years, remove only crossing shoots.

Tip-prune the main branches on the stronger side

PRECAUTIONS

• Carry out work only on small trees. Consult a professional tree surgeon for larger ones.

• Work from the ground whenever possible, and take care if using ladders or climbing the tree.

• Never attempt to climb the tree when the bark is wet and slippery.

• Keep the area around the tree clear of equipment, children, and pets.

• If using a chain saw, do so from the ground, and never on branches above waist height.

• Before undertaking any work, always consult your local council. The tree may be legally protected, and you may need permission for felling or even simply to remove branches.

CUTTING OFF A BRANCH

It is vital to exercise particular care when cutting a branch off a tree. It can be dangerous and, if done incorrectly, may damage the tree. A branch over 30cm (12in) in circumference is best removed in stages. The use of two cuts prevents any tearing of the bark when the cut portion falls. Make the final cut just outside the branch collar, the swelling at the branch base, where the tree's natural defences are located. Keeping this cut clean and smooth minimizes the risk of infection entering the tree, so clean the edges of the cut with a sharp knife. Do not paint the cut surface.

Top cut
Undercut
Final cut
Branch collar

WHERE TO CUT
When making final cuts, avoid damaging the branch collar at the base of the branch, since this area protects the tree from infection.

1 Using a pruning saw, make the first cut from beneath the branch, about 30cm (12in) from the trunk, and only about one-quarter of the way through the branch.

2 Remove the outer portion of the branch by cutting through from above, about 2.5cm (1in) further from the trunk than the original cut.

3 To cut off the stub, make a small undercut from below, then saw from above, angling the saw slightly away from the trunk, until the two cuts meet.

CUTTING DOWN A SMALL TREE

Tree felling can be a very hazardous activity. If you have to cut down a tree in your garden, tackle only those up to 5m (15ft) tall. To fell larger trees, you will need to seek the services of a professional tree surgeon. A bow saw is useful for felling small trees, but it may be difficult to use in confined areas. Trees are best taken down in stages. Before you begin, ensure that there is sufficient space for the tree to fall safely. Remove the larger branches, then make three cuts as shown below, the first two on the side where the tree is to fall. Finally, dig out the stump and roots.

1 Using a bow saw, make an angled cut one-third into the trunk on the side where the tree is to fall. The cut should be about 1m (3ft) from the ground.

2 Make a horizontal cut to meet the base of the angled cut. Remove the wedge of timber. This will ensure that the tree falls in the planned direction when cut.

3 Make the final cut on the opposite side, just above the wedge. Push the tree as it starts to fall. Dig a trench around the remaining stump and dig or pull it out.

PRUNING FOR SPECIAL EFFECT

CERTAIN TREES GROWN FOR their ornamental shoots and bark can be greatly enhanced by special pruning techniques, such as pollarding and coppicing. These encourage the production of vigorous new growth, and also restrict the size of the plant, keeping the ornamental features at eye level. Some evergreen trees, such as hollies (*Ilex*), bay (*Laurus*), and yew (*Taxus*), are suited to training as standards (*see pp.52–53*). Remove the lower branches to the desired height, then prune in the spring before growth starts until you achieve the desired shape. Trim mature plants regularly but lightly in summer.

CREATING MULTI-STEMMED TREES

Many trees naturally produce several stems from the base; for those that do not, you can encourage a multi-stemmed habit by pruning. This is particularly desirable for trees with ornamental bark or shoots, since it shows them to best effect. Examples of trees that are suited to growing as multi-stemmed specimens include *Acer davidii* and other snake-bark maples, birches (*Betula*), *Cercis*, and *Lagerstroemia*.

▶ MULTI-STEMMED MAPLE
Growing Acer pensylvanicum *'Erythrocladum' as a multi-stemmed tree makes it stronger and creates more young shoots for winter effect.*

Remove most of the main stem and branches

Side shoots will grow from the main shoots

Retain vigorous shoots

Remove any regrowth at base

Cut cleanly across the stem

Remove weaker shoots

YEAR 1, WINTER
Cut the main stem of a 2-year-old tree at least 8cm (3in) from the ground, more if desired. Trim sharp edges.

YEAR 2, WINTER
Choose approximately 3 strong, well-spaced shoots of equal vigour. Cut all other shoots back to the base.

YEAR 3, WINTER
Allow side shoots to develop, cutting only the lower ones if you want clear stems. Remove any suckers that may appear.

POLLARDING AND COPPICING

These pruning techniques restrict growth and encourage the production of vigorous young shoots for winter or foliage effect. Among the best trees for pollarding are forms of the white willow (*Salix alba*). To pollard a tree, first let it develop until well established and growing strongly. Just before growth starts in spring, reduce it to the required stem height by sawing across the main stem. Cut the remaining shoots back to 2.5–8cm (1–3in) long.

Coppicing is similar, but the tree is cut down to just above ground level. This creates a shrubby effect, with many shoots arising from the base. It is usually used on hazel (*Corylus avellana*), but can also be applied to some large trees, such as *Paulownia tomentosa* and *Ailanthus altissima*, encouraging the production of vigorous shoots and very large leaves.

▲ STRIKING STEMS
Regular pollarding of the willow Salix alba *'Britzensis' produces a head of vigorous red shoots, which are a striking feature in the garden in winter and early spring.*

◄ CUTTING BACK
The variegated forms of Acer negundo *can be cut back hard in spring to encourage a bushy habit and to restrict their size.*

VARIEGATED NEW LEAVES
The maple Acer negundo *'Flamingo' responds extremely well to hard pruning. Shown here pollarded to a low stem, it produces numerous vigorous shoots that bear large, attractively variegated young leaves, making a more handsome plant than if left unpruned.*

POLLARDING TIPS

• Prune established pollards every 2–3 years.
• Carry out pollarding in early spring so that the ornamental effects can be enjoyed over winter.
• Remove any shoots on the main stem below the head or at the base of the tree as they appear.
• When growth starts, the shoots may be overcrowded. Remove some if necessary to create an even head of branches.

PESTS, DISEASES, AND DISORDERS

MOST TREES enjoy a healthy life. Some, however will suffer at some time from pests, diseases, or disorders. Pests are generally insects or other creatures that feed on parts of a tree, diseases are caused by fungi, bacteria, or viruses, and disorders are usually the result of poor growing conditions. A healthy, well-maintained tree will be considerably more resistant to problems of all kinds than one that is in poor condition.

PREVENTING PROBLEMS

Buy a good, healthy specimen that is suited to the conditions in your garden. Plant it correctly, and water and weed regularly. Prune as little as possible, use clean, sharp tools, and avoid wounding stems (for example, when using a lawn mower). If diseased material is found on other woody plants in the garden, remove and burn it straight away. Check regularly for signs of pests and diseases, and take immediate action if a problem occurs.

MOTTLING
Tiny red spider mites feed off the foliage, causing a dull mottling on the surface and early leaf fall. Spray leaves with a suitable pesticide.

Susceptible trees: maples (*Acer*), crab apples (*Malus*), spruce (*Picea*), and willows (*Salix*).

Distorted growth

STUNTED LEAVES
Aphids (greenfly and blackfly) suck sap and leave a sticky deposit. Spray small trees with a suitable pesticide as soon as seen.

Susceptible trees: maples (*Acer*), hawthorns (*Crataegus*), beech (*Fagus*), crab apples (*Malus*), *Prunus*, *Sorbus*.

PIMPLES
Unsightly growths (galls) form, usually on the leaves, as a response to feeding by insects or mites. No effective control but no real harm is done.

Susceptible trees: maples (*Acer*), beech (*Fagus*), *Gleditsia triacanthos* 'Sunburst', oaks (*Quercus*), elms (*Ulmus*).

CHEWED LEAVES
Caterpillars can quickly eat through foliage. Collect up any caterpillars on the tree's leaves; alternatively, use chemical sprays for serious infestations.

Susceptible trees: maples (*Acer*), hornbeams (*Carpinus*), bay (*Laurus*), crab apples (*Malus*), *Prunus*, *Sorbus*.

SHRIVELLED LEAVES
Drought causes leaves to wilt, shrivel, or colour early. Prevent this by watering the tree regularly, especially in the year after planting. Mulch newly planted trees.

Susceptible trees: all trees may be affected, especially those that have been newly planted or grown in containers.

CONGESTED SHOOTS
Dense clusters of congested shoots are produced on branches in response to insect or fungal attack. Cut back affected shoots to normal wood.

Susceptible trees: birches (*Betula*), hornbeams (*Carpinus*), *Prunus*.

PUSTULES ON BARK
Orange-pink spots of the coral spot fungus usually appear on dead shoots but can harm live wood. Cut affected shoots back to healthy wood.

Dead bark covered in pustules

Susceptible trees: horse chestnuts (*Aesculus*), hornbeams (*Carpinus*), *Cercis*, magnolias, sumachs (*Rhus*).

FUNGUS
White growth and black strands under the bark of trunks and roots indicate honey fungus. Remove and destroy infected root systems.

Susceptible trees: Birches (*Betula*), *Chamaecyparis*, *Cupressus*, magnolias, crab apples (*Malus*), *Prunus*, pears (*Pyrus*).

RUPTURED BARK
Rapid uptake of water after a prolonged drought causes stems to swell suddenly, splitting the bark. Water regularly in dry spells.

Susceptible trees: all trees are affected, but especially those growing in containers or in soil that dries out quickly.

WOUNDED BARK
Mechanical damage or incorrect or unclean pruning cuts can damage trunks. Ensure stakes do not rub, and prune trees correctly (pp.51, 55).

Susceptible trees: all trees are affected, but especially those grown in grass, which are liable to damage by lawn mowers.

Stem may split and eventually die back

CRACKED STEM
Extremely low temperatures or sudden temperature changes cause stems to freeze and split. Grow tender trees in a sheltered position.

Susceptible trees: many trees are affected, but especially young or slightly tender ones, and in particular those growing in exposed sites.

OTHER COMMON PROBLEMS

LEAVES AND FLOWERS

White powder on leaves Powdery mildew causes leaves to fall early. Water well and spray with fungicide.

Leaf spots Bacteria or fungi cause blotches on leaves. Remove and burn affected foliage as soon as seen.

Eaten flower buds Bullfinches have a tendency to eat the flower buds of some trees in winter, especially those of *Prunus*.

SHOOTS

Eaten bark and shoots Deer and rabbits eat the shoots, bark, and foliage of trees, so use a stem guard for protection (*p.48*).

White fluff on conifers A sign of aphid-like insects (adelgids), which suck sap from the leaves and shoots. Spray with a pesticide.

Brown scales with white egg deposits Scale insects feed on the shoots and leaves of many trees. Control by spraying with a pesticide.

RECOMMENDED SMALL TREES

THE SYMBOLS AND HEIGHTS given in this plant directory apply to all trees described in the entry unless otherwise stated. If lime-free soil is not specified, assume the tree is suitable for any reasonably good, well-drained soil.

▣ *Shade tolerant* ▣ *Suitable for sun or partial shade* ▣ *Best in full sun* ◊ *Tolerates dry soil* ◊ *Requires moist, well-drained soil* ◊ *Tolerates wet soil* ✻✻✻ *Fully hardy* ✻✻ *Frost hardy* H *Approximate maximum height growing in cultivation in reasonable conditions* ♥ *RHS Award of Garden Merit*

A

Abies koreana
(Korean fir)
Evergreen, narrowly conical conifer with densely arranged, glossy dark green leaves, bright blue-white beneath. Small, blue-purple cones are borne even on small plants. It is best grown in lime-free soil.
▣ ◊ ✻✻✻ H 10m (30ft)

ABIES KOREANA

Abies lasiocarpa var arizonica 'Compacta'
This slow-growing, very compact, narrowly columnar evergreen conifer needs lime-free soil. It has dense, bright blue-grey foliage.
▣ ◊ ✻✻✻ H 5m (15ft)

Aesculus × neglecta 'Erythroblastos' ♥
(Sunrise horse chestnut)
Deciduous, broadly columnar tree (*p.26*). The leaves are brilliant pink in spring, turning green flushed yellow then green in summer. The creamy white flowers, which are borne in late spring, are inconspicuous.
▣ ◊ ✻✻✻ H 8m (25ft)

Aesculus pavia
(Red buckeye)
Deciduous, broadly conical tree (*p.30*), which bears tubular red flowers in early summer. 'Atrosanguinea' has deep red flowers. The forms of *A. × mutabilis*, such as 'Induta' and 'Penduliflora',

are similar but more bushy, with pink flowers marked with yellow.
▣ ✻✻✻ H 6m (20ft)

Albizia julibrissin f. rosea ♥
(Pink siris, Silk tree)
Deciduous, rounded to spreading tree. It has elegant, fern-like leaves and showy pink powder-puff-like clusters in summer.
▣ ◊ ✻✻ H 6m (20ft)

AESCULUS PAVIA
'ATROSANGUINEA'

◄ MALUS 'RED JADE' *The white flowers of this crab apple are magnificent in late spring.*

ACER (MAPLE)

Maples form a diverse group, from shrubs to large trees. All have excellent foliage, and provide some of the best trees for autumn colour. Many also have interesting bark or shoots, or an attractive habit. The following are all deciduous, and the majority are rounded or spreading.

🏵 ◊ ✳✳✳ H 10m (30ft)

Maples with attractive bark or shoots

The snake-bark maples are fast-growing trees with green- and white-streaked bark and good autumn colour. They include *A. capillipes* ♀ (*p.17*), *A. crataegifolium* (Hawthorn maple), *A. davidii* (some of which, including 'Ernest Wilson', colour orange in autumn), *A. grosseri* var. *hersii* ♀, and *A. rufinerve* ♀. Another attractive snake-bark maple is *A. pensylvanicum* (Moosewood, *p.29*), with yellow leaves in autumn; 'Erythrocladum' (*p.56*) has bright pink winter shoots.

Other maples grown for their bark or shoots include: *A. buergerianum* (Trident maple), with orange-brown flaking bark and red autumn colour; *A. griseum* (Paper-bark maple, *p.28*), with striking peeling cinnamon-brown bark; *A. palmatum* 'Senkaki', syn. 'Sango-kaku' (Coral-bark maple, *pp.28, 38*), with shoots coral-red in winter; *A. triflorum* (*p.27*), with pale grey-brown peeling bark and brilliant orange autumn colour.

Maples grown for foliage

A. cappadocicum 'Aureum' ♀ has yellow foliage, which turns a little greener in summer. *A. japonicum* 'Aconitifolium' ♀, with deeply cut leaves, is slightly shrubby, to 5m (15ft); 'Vitifolium' ♀ is larger, with bigger, less divided leaves. Both turn bright red in autumn. *A. negundo* 'Auratum' has yellow foliage; 'Elegans' has green leaves with yellow margins, while in 'Flamingo' (*pp.17, 57*) the edges have a strong pink flush when young; 'Variegatum' has leaves that are edged white.

The foliage of *A. palmatum* (*pp.17, 34*) turns orange, red, or yellow in autumn. Selections include 'Atropurpureum', with purple leaves; 'Linearilobum', with the leaves cut into slender lobes; 'Ôsakazuki' ♀, with large leaves, red in autumn; and 'Shishigashira', broadly columnar, to 5m (15ft), with small, sharply toothed leaves. *A. pseudoplatanus* 'Brilliantissimum' (*p.40*) and 'Prinz Handjery' have bright pink young foliage, purple below when mature in the latter. *A. rubrum* 'Schlesingeri' colours early in autumn, very bright red. *A. shirasawanum* 'Aureum' (*pp.8, 27*) has bright yellow foliage. *A. tataricum* subsp. *ginnala* ♀ has glossy leaves, turning red in autumn.

Maples grown for their habit

Several forms of Japanese maple, *A. palmatum*, are occasionally grown as weeping trees, 2.5–3m (8–10ft) tall. Dissectum Group cultivars have finely cut leaves turning orange to red in autumn, such as 'Crimson Queen' ♀, with red-purple foliage, or the green-leaved var. *dissectum* ♀. *A. platanoides* 'Globosum' is a lollipop-shaped tree reaching only about 6m (20ft). *A. saccharum* 'Newton Sentry' is narrowly columnar, with orange-red autumn colour.

ACER NEGUNDO
'FLAMINGO'

ACER PALMATUM

ACER PALMATUM
'ATROPURPUREUM'

ARBUTUS × *ANDRACHNOIDES* ♀

Alnus glutinosa 'Imperialis' ♀

This form of the common alder is a graceful, broadly conical deciduous tree, which has finely cut dark green leaves arranged on slightly drooping shoots. Needs permanently moist soil.
▣ ◊ ✳✳✳ H 10m (30ft)

Alnus incana 'Aurea'

Deciduous, broadly columnar tree with orange-pink shoots and young catkins in winter that create the effect of a pink haze. It has yellow-green young foliage. 'Pendula', another form of *A. incana*, is weeping in habit.
▣ ◊◊ ✳✳✳ H 10m (30ft)

Amelanchier

(Serviceberry)
Deciduous, rounded or spreading, sometimes shrubby trees that require lime-free soil. They have attractive young foliage that turns orange to red in autumn, white spring flowers, and blue-black fruits. *A. arborea* and *A. lamarckii* ♀ (*p.22*) both have silvery young leaves. *A.* × *grandiflora*, including its forms 'Autumn Brilliance', 'Ballerina' ♀, and 'Rubescens' (with pink flower buds), as well as *A. laevis*, have bronze young foliage.
▣▉◊ ✳✳✳ H 8–10m (25–30ft)

Aralia elata ♀

(Japanese angelica tree)
Deciduous, suckering shrub or broadly columnar tree with spiny stems, large divided leaves, and a gaunt winter profile. Small white flowers appear in late summer as the leaves turn orange, yellow, and purple; small black fruits follow. The similar *A. spinosa* flowers in early summer.
▣ ◊ ✳✳✳ H 10m (30ft)

Arbutus

These spreading, evergreen trees, sometimes shrubby in habit, produce particularly attractive fruits and bark. *A.* × *andrachnoides* ♀ has cinnamon-brown peeling bark and small white flowers from autumn to spring. *A. unedo* ♀ (Strawberry tree) bears small white flowers, pink in f. *rubra*, and strawberry-like fruits in autumn and winter. It also has rough-textured, reddish brown bark.
▣ ◊ ✳✳✳ H 8m (25ft)

B

Betula pendula

(Common birch)
Narrowly conical, deciduous tree with white bark and weeping shoots. 'Laciniata' ♀ produces finely cut leaves, 'Tristis' ♀ has long, pendulous shoots. 'Youngii', to 8m (25ft), has a mushroom-shaped head, and shoots to the ground.
▣ ◊ ✳✳✳ H 20m (70ft) or more

Betula populifolia

(Grey birch, White birch)
Deciduous, narrowly conical tree with reddish brown bark becoming white or grey. The slender shoots are somewhat pendulous, and the glossy dark green leaves turn yellow in autumn.
▣ ◊ ✳✳✳ H 10m (30ft)

Betula utilis var. jacquemontii

(Himalayan birch)
Vigorous deciduous, narrowly columnar tree (*pp.29, 36*) with white bark. It bears long catkins in spring and has golden yellow autumn colour. 'Jermyns' ♀ is a form with particularly attractive, pure white bark.
▣ ◊ ✳✳✳ H 15m (50ft)

Buddleja alternifolia ♀

Deciduous, weeping shrub (*p.10*), which is sometimes available as a weeping standard. It has slender, grey-green leaves. In early summer, clusters of fragrant lilac flowers are borne along the branches. Mature specimens have attractive flaking bark.
▣ ◊ ✳✳✳ H 3m (10ft)

BETULA PENDULA 'TRISTIS' ♀

C

Calocedrus decurrens 'Berrima Gold'

Evergreen, narrowly columnar conifer, a slow-growing form of the large incense cedar. It has bright yellow, aromatic foliage turning orange-yellow in winter, and orange bark.
◪ ◊ ✳✳✳ H 6m (20ft)

Caragana arborescens

(Pea tree)
Deciduous, broadly columnar shrub with divided leaves and yellow flowers in spring. The following are usually grown as standards: 'Lorbergii' ♀, with slender, arching shoots and very finely cut leaves, and 'Pendula', which is not usually above 1.5m (5ft), often less, and has stiff, strongly weeping shoots.
◪ ◊ ✳✳✳ H 3m (10ft)

Carpinus

(Hornbeam)
Hornbeams are deciduous trees grown for their elegant habit, foliage, autumn colour, and fruits. C. betulus

CATALPA BIGNONIOIDES
'AUREA' ♀

(Common hornbeam) has sharply toothed leaves turning yellow in autumn, and is 10m (30ft) tall. 'Columnaris' (p.12) is compact and narrowly columnar; 'Fastigiata' ♀ becomes large and requires pruning to keep it narrow, while 'Frans Fontaine' retains its narrow shape; 'Pendula' is a mushroom-headed tree, to 2.5m (8ft) tall, the branches weeping to the ground.
C. caroliniana (American hornbeam, Blue beech, Musclewood) is larger, occasionally reaching 12m (40ft) tall, sometimes shrubby, and rounded to spreading. Its autumn leaves are yellow or orange, and green fruit clusters hang beneath the branches in summer, turning yellow-brown.
◪◪ ◊ ✳✳✳

Catalpa bignonioides 'Aurea' ♀

(Indian bean tree)
Deciduous, rounded to spreading tree with large golden leaves, which appear late, and often bearing large heads of white flowers in summer, followed by long, slender, persistent pods.
◪◪ ✳✳✳ H 8m (25ft)

Cercis

Deciduous, rounded to spreading trees with small, usually pink flowers that appear before the leaves open. Mature trees often bear flowers on the main trunk and branches. C. canadensis 'Forest Pansy' ♀ (Eastern redbud) has purple foliage. C. chinensis reaches only 6m (20ft) high, with glossy foliage, and 'Avondale' is even more compact at 3m (10ft).

C. siliquastrum (Judas tree, p.11) produces pink or occasionally white flowers.
◪ ◊ ✳✳ H 10m (30ft)

Chamaecyparis

(Cypress)
This is a group of narrowly columnar conifers. Forms of C. lawsoniana (Lawson cypress) include 'Columnaris' and 'Ellwoodii' ♀, both with blue-grey foliage. Selections of C. obtusa include 'Crippsii' ♀ (p.13), with sprays of golden-yellow foliage, and 'Tetragona Aurea' ♀, which has clustered golden to bronze-yellow foliage. C. pisifera 'Boulevard' has soft blue-grey leaves. C. thyoides 'Andeleyensis' is dense and narrow in habit, with blue-green foliage, and reaches 5–6m (15–20ft) tall.
◪ ◊ ✳✳✳ H 10m (30ft)

Chionanthus

(Fringe tree)
Deciduous or evergreen trees grown for their flowers and fruits. C. retusus, which is deciduous, has fragrant white summer flowers, small blue-black fruits that follow in

CHAMAECYPARIS OBTUSA
'CRIPPSII' ♀

CHIONANTHUS VIRGINICUS

autumn, and attractive flaking bark. *C. virginicus*, also deciduous, is grown for its large clusters of fragrant white flowers in summer, followed by small, blue-black fruits. Needs lime-free soil.

▣ ✳✳✳ H 3–4m (10–12ft)

Cordyline australis ♀
(New Zealand cabbage palm) Evergreen, palm-like tree (*p.35*) with a dense head of slender leaves. Large clusters of small white fragrant summer flowers are followed by tiny white or blue-tinged berries. 'Albertii' ♀ has cream leaves edged pink; 'Atropurpurea' has purple-flushed foliage; 'Torbay Dazzler' has leaves striped cream; 'Variegata' has leaves striped creamy white.

▣ ◊ ✳✳ H 10m (30ft)

Cotoneaster
The following cotoneasters may be available as weeping standards: *C.* 'Herbstfeuer' (syn. *C.* 'Autumn Fire'), with glossy evergreen leaves and red berries; *C. integrifolius* (syn. *C. microphyllus*), with tiny dark green evergreen

CORNUS (DOGWOOD)

Dogwoods are grown for their flowers, elegant habit, and autumn colour. They are mainly rounded and spreading deciduous shrubs and small trees.

▣ ◊ ✳✳✳

Flowering dogwoods
The flowering dogwoods are those with very large bracts. *C. capitata* is evergreen, but is suitable only for mild areas. It reaches 10m (30ft) tall and across. The bracts emerge creamy yellow and may become flushed pink. Bears strawberry-like fruits in autumn. *C.* 'Eddie's White Wonder' ♀ has white bracts and needs a lime-free soil. It reaches 6m (20ft). *C. florida* is a spreading tree, sometimes shrubby, growing to 6m (20ft). There are many forms, with bracts ranging from deep pink in 'Cherokee Chief' ♀ to white in 'White Cloud', opening in late spring to early summer. Needs a lime-free soil. *C. kousa* is similar to *C. florida*, but will grow in alkaline soil. It has creamy bracts in early to midsummer, peeling bark, and red autumn

CORNUS FLORIDA 'CHEROKEE CHIEF' ♀

CORNUS MAS ♀

colour. It reaches 6m (20ft). Among the best forms are var. *chinensis* ♀, with large bracts, and 'Satomi' ♀, with red bracts. *C.* 'Norman Hadden' ♀ has creamy bracts turning to deep pink over a long period, followed by strawberry-like red fruits.

Other dogwoods
C. alternifolia 'Argentea' may be grown as a tree, but is more often a shrub, to about 3m (10ft). It has distinctive tiered branches, leaves broadly edged creamy white, and small white summer flowers. *C. controversa* 'Variegata' ♀ is similar but is larger, to 8m (25ft) tall and across, and with larger leaves. *C. macrophylla* is broadly conical, to 10m (30ft), with bold dark green leaves, broad heads of small white flowers in late summer, and small blue-black fruits. *C. mas* ♀ (Cornelian cherry) is often shrubby but may be tree-like, up to 8m (25ft). Small yellow flowers open on the bare branches in late winter, and are often followed by edible red fruits.

CRATAEGUS LAEVIGATA
'PAUL'S SCARLET' ♀

leaves, rigid, arching shoots, and crimson-pink fruits. C. 'Hybridus Pendulus' (syn. C. salicifolius 'Pendulus') is semi-evergreen, to 2m (6ft), with profuse red berries.
🅩 ◊�◔ ✳✳✳ H 1.2–1.5m (4–5ft)

Crataegus
(Hawthorn)
Hawthorns are deciduous, rounded to spreading trees, usually thorny and with white flowers in early summer. C. crus-galli (Cockspur thorn) has long, curved spines, persistent red fruits, and red autumn colour. C. laciniata (p.38) has lobed dark green leaves and orange-red fruits. Forms of C. laevigata (Midland hawthorn) are grown for their flowers, such as 'Crimson Cloud', red with a white eye, and 'Paul's Scarlet' ♀, double and deep pink. The semi-evergreen C. × lavallei 'Carrierei' ♀ has orange-red fruits lasting into winter. C. monogyna 'Biflora' (Glastonbury thorn) often bears flowers in winter. C. pedicellata has large red

fruits. For red autumn colour, C. persimilis 'Prunifolia' ♀ (p.24) is quite spectacular. C. phaenopyrum (Washington thorn) has maple-like leaves, red in autumn, and produces small red fruits.
🅩 ◊◔ ✳✳✳ H 8m (25ft)

Cupressus
(Cypress)
These are evergreen, narrowly conical conifers. C. arizonica 'Pyramidalis' ♀ may exceed 10m (30ft), but it is compact with attractive blue-grey foliage. Forms of the Italian cypress, C. sempervirens, like 'Green Pencil' and 'Stricta' ♀, 6m (20ft), make good dark green, formal specimens. 'Swane's Gold' ♀, to 6m (20ft), has golden foliage.
🅩 ◊ ✳✳✳

Cydonia oblonga
(Common quince)
This is a deciduous, rounded to spreading tree with large, pale pink flowers in late spring and large fragrant, yellow fruits. 'Lusitanica' and 'Vranja' ♀ are grown for their edible fruits.
🅩 ◊ ✳✳✳ H 5m (15ft)

EMBOTHRIUM COCCINEUM

ERIOBOTRYA JAPONICA ♀

E

Elaeagnus angustifolia ♀
(Oleaster, Russian olive)
Deciduous, spreading shrub or tree (p.32), valued since it grows in poor, dry, salty soils. It has slender, willow-like, silvery leaves and tiny scented yellow summer flowers.
🅩 ◊ ✳✳✳ H 8m (25ft)

Embothrium coccineum
(Chilean fire bush)
Deciduous or semi-evergreen, broadly columnar tree that needs lime-free soil. It bears showy, bright red flowers in late spring and early summer among the narrow dark green leaves. 'Norquinco' ♀ flowers very profusely.
🅩 ◊ ✳✳✳ H 10m (30ft)

Eriobotrya japonica ♀
(Loquat)
Evergreen, rounded to spreading tree or shrub. Its small fragrant white flowers open in autumn or winter. Where summers are hot or winters mild, it will produce edible, orange-yellow fruits.
🅩 ◊ ✳✳ H 8m (25ft)

Eucryphia glutinosa
This deciduous or semi-evergreen, broadly columnar tree needs lime-free soil. It produces glossy, dark green leaves, orange-red in autumn, and large white, slightly fragrant flowers that open in mid- to late summer.
◫ ◊ ✳✳✳ H 10m (30ft)

F

Fagus sylvatica
(Common beech)
This deciduous tree has several forms that are suitable for small gardens. 'Aurea Pendula' is slender and narrowly columnar, with pendulous branches hanging against the trunk and yellow foliage. 'Dawyck Gold' ✿ is also narrowly columnar, with yellow foliage becoming green, then turning yellow again in autumn. 'Purple Fountain' ✿ is similar to 'Aurea Pendula', but with purple foliage, while 'Purpurea Pendula' (p.20) is weeping, to only 3m (10ft), and has deep purple leaves.
◫ ◊ ✳✳✳ H 10m (30ft)

FRANKLINIA ALATAMAHA

Ficus carica
(Common fig)
This deciduous tree, often shrubby, has a spreading head of bold, deeply lobed leaves. The edible fruits can be up to 10cm (4in) long. 'Brown Turkey' has purple fruits. In cool climates it is best grown against a sunny wall.
◫ ◊ ✳✳✳ H 5m (15ft)

Franklinia alatamaha
(Franklin tree)
Rounded or spreading deciduous tree or shrub. This has glossy dark green leaves, which are bright red in autumn. In late summer, large, cup-shaped, fragrant white flowers open. It needs hot summers to thrive.
◫ ◊ ✳✳✳ H 5m (15ft)

G

Genista aetnensis ✿
(Mount Etna broom)
Almost leafless, the green stems of this rounded to spreading, deciduous tree give it an evergreen appearance. In late summer, it is covered in small, fragrant, bright yellow flowers.
◫ ◊ ✳✳✳ H 8m (25ft)

Gleditsia triacanthos 'Sunburst' ✿
This deciduous tree is broadly conical in habit. It is fast growing and may exceed 10m (30ft) tall. It is grown for its elegant, fern-like foliage, which is bright yellow when young and dark green in maturity, turning yellow in autumn. Unlike most other gleditsias, this form is thornless.
◫ ◊ ✳✳✳ H 10m (30ft)

H

Halesia
(Silverbell, Snowdrop tree)
These are deciduous trees that require a lime-free soil. Normally broadly conical in outline, they branch low from the base. In late spring, they bear white, snowdrop-like flowers, and in autumn they produce green, winged fruits. H. diptera is about 8m (25ft), and frequently shrubby; H. monticola often exceeds 10m (30ft). It has a pink-flowered form, f. rosea.
◫ ◊ ✳✳✳

Hydrangea paniculata
Vigorous, spreading, deciduous shrub that is sometimes available as a standard. Produces attractive, large flowerheads in late summer and autumn. Recommended selections include 'Grandiflora' ✿ and 'Unique' ✿, with large white flowerheads turning pink. 'Praecox' ✿ flowers relatively early, and 'Tardiva' is a late-flowering form.
◫ ◊ ✳✳✳ H 3m (10ft)

HALESIA MONTICOLA

ILEX (HOLLY)

Hollies include some of the most popular evergreens, valued for their foliage and berries. Unless otherwise stated, the following are female with red berries, and narrowly conical in habit. Berries are only produced if a male plant is growing nearby.
▣ ◊ ✻✻✻ H 5–6m (15–20ft)

Common hollies
Forms of *I. aquifolium* ♀ (Common or English holly) include 'Argentea Marginata Pendula', weeping, to 2.5m (8ft), with cream-edged leaves; 'Golden Milkboy' ♀, male, with leaves blotched yellow; 'Green Pillar' ♀, a narrowly upright form; 'Handsworth New Silver' ♀, with purple shoots and white-edged leaves; 'Madame Briot' ♀, with purple stems and yellow-edged leaves, to 10m (30ft); the male 'Ovata Aurea', with purple shoots and gold-edged leaves; 'Pyramidalis Fructu Luteo' ♀, with yellow berries and mostly spineless leaves; and 'Silver Milkmaid' ♀, with spiny white-blotched leaves.
　Similar to common hollies are forms of *I.* × *altaclerensis*. Selections include 'Belgica

ILEX PEDUNCULOSA

ILEX AQUIFOLIUM 'SILVER MILKMAID' ♀

Aurea' ♀, with yellow-edged leaves, the margin becoming creamy white, to 10m (30ft) or more; 'Camelliifolia Variegata', with leaves broadly edged yellow; 'Golden King' ♀ (*p.33*), with yellow-edged leaves; and 'Lawsoniana' ♀, with leaves blotched yellow and pale green in the centre.

Other hollies
I. × *attenuata* (Topel holly) is bushy, with narrow, spiny leaves and red berries on female plants. *I. latifolia*, to 8m (25ft), has long, bold, dark green leaves; red fruits on female plants may persist in winter. *I.* × *koehneana* is similar with smaller, spinier leaves. *I.* 'Nellie R. Stevens' is conical, to 7m (22ft), with very spiny leaves and red fruits. *I. opaca* (American holly), to 10m (30ft), has matt to glossy, pale to dark green, spiny foliage. It prefers hot summers and lime-free soil. *I. pedunculosa*, 7m (22ft), has wavy-edged, spineless leaves, bronze when young, and long-stalked red berries on female plants.

J

Juniperus chinensis
(Chinese juniper)
Evergreen conifer with forms including 'Aurea' ♀, which is narrow and slow growing, with bright yellow foliage; 'Kaizuka' ♀ (Hollywood juniper), to 6m (20ft), with irregularly spreading shoots and profuse, bloomy berries; 'Spartan', which is a narrow column of bright green.
▣ ◊ ✻✻✻ H 10m (30ft)

Juniperus communis
(Common juniper)
This is usually a shrub but has some tree-like forms, such as the narrowly columnar 'Hibernica' ♀, which often becomes untidy with age; 'Sentinel' is slower growing, narrower, and more compact.
▣ ◊ ✻✻✻ H 5m (15ft)

Juniperus scopulorum 'Skyrocket'
One of the narrowest of all conifers, with blue-grey evergreen foliage.
▣ ◊ ✻✻✻ H 6m (20ft)

KOELREUTERIA PANICULATA ♀

K

Koelreuteria paniculata ♀
(Golden rain tree, Pride of
India)
Deciduous tree of spreading
habit, with leaves emerging
bronze-red, turning green,
then orange or yellow in
autumn. Large clusters of
yellow flowers open in
summer, turning to green or
pink, later with brown,
lantern-like fruits. 'Fastigiata'
has upright branches.
▨ ◊ ✱✱✱ H 10m (30ft)

L

+ Laburnocytisus 'Adamii'
A combination of a laburnum
and a broom (Cytisus)
produced by grafting, this
curious deciduous tree is
rounded to spreading in shape
and produces three types of
flowers: yellow and
laburnum-like; purple and
pea-like, resembling broom;
and purple-pink flushed with
yellow, a mixture of the two.
▨ ◊ ✱✱✱ H 6m (20ft)

LAGERSTROEMIA INDICA
'SEMINOLE'

LAURUS NOBILIS 'AUREA' ♀

Laburnum
These deciduous trees are
excellent as specimens for
small gardens. They are
grown for their long,
pendulous clusters of bright
yellow flowers in late spring
and early summer. All parts of
laburnums are highly toxic if
they are eaten. L. alpinum
'Pendulum' is a weeping tree,
1.5m (5ft) tall. L. × watereri
'Vossii' ♀ (p.25) is broadly
columnar and considerably
taller, to 8m (25ft) high.
▨ ◊ ✱✱✱

Lagerstroemia indica ♀
(Crape myrtle)
Deciduous, broadly columnar
tree or shrub with peeling
bark and profuse flowers in
large clusters in summer and
autumn. Flowers may be
white to pink, red, or purple.
'Seminole' is compact, to 3m
(10ft), with mid-pink flowers
produced from midsummer to
early autumn.
▨ ◊ ✱✱ H 8m (25ft)

Laurus nobilis
(Bay laurel, Sweet bay)
Evergreen, broadly conical
tree, popular for its strongly

aromatic foliage, used in
cooking. The yellow-leaved
'Aurea' ♀ is slower growing,
reaching about 8m (25ft).
▨ ◊ ✱✱✱ H 12m (40ft)

Ligustrum lucidum ♀
(Chinese privet)
Evergreen, broadly conical
tree. Bold foliage is enhanced
in late summer and autumn
by large clusters of tiny white
flowers, followed by small,
blue-black fruits. It has two
variegated forms that are
smaller, to about 8m (25ft):
'Excelsum Superbum' ♀, with
yellow-margined foliage; and
'Tricolor', which has pink-
edged leaves when young,
turning creamy white.
▨ ◊ ✱✱✱ H 15m (50ft)

Luma apiculata ♀
(syn. Myrtus luma)
This evergreen tree is best in
areas where winters are mild.
Rounded to spreading, it has
glossy, aromatic foliage,
cinnamon-brown bark that
peels to leave creamy white
patches, and white flowers in
summer and autumn.
▨ ◊ ✱✱ H 10m (30ft) or more

LIGUSTRUM LUCIDUM
'EXCELSUM SUPERBUM' ♀

M

Maackia amurensis
·This makes a small, rounded and spreading deciduous tree, with dark green, divided leaves, grey when they first open. The small white, or slightly blue-tinged, fragrant pea-like flowers appear in dense, upright spikes in mid- to late summer, and are followed by flattened seed pods. Grows best in areas with hot summers.
▣ ◊ ✱✱✱ H 8m (25ft)

Mespilus germanica
(Medlar)
Deciduous, rounded to spreading tree of picturesque habit when mature. Large white flowers, sometimes pink-tinged, open at the ends of short shoots in late spring. Bold green leaves turn yellow-brown in autumn, and round, russet-coloured fruits ripen at the same time.
▣ ◊ ✱✱✱ H 6m (20ft)

Morus alba
(White mulberry)
Deciduous, spreading tree with heart-shaped, bright green leaves that turn yellow in autumn. It bears insipid-tasting white fruits in late summer. 'Pendula' is an excellent form for small gardens. It makes a mound of weeping shoots, arching to the ground with bright green foliage, sometimes reaching 5m (15ft) tall and across. It is especially attractive when bearing its small but striking, edible red fruits along the drooping branches.
▣ ◊ ✱✱✱ H 10m (30ft)

MAGNOLIA

Unrivalled in the size and spectacle of their usually fragrant flowers, magnolias are splendid trees. Some kinds, such as *M. denudata* ♛ (Yulan) and *M. obovata* ♛ (syn. *M. hypoleuca*), need lime-free soil.
▣ ◊ ✱✱✱

Spring-flowering magnolias
For large white flowers, try *M. denudata* ♛ (Yulan), or the more upright *M. kobus* and *M. salicifolia* ♛, with selections like 'Kewensis' and 'Wada's Memory' ♛ (p.25). All grow to about 10m (30ft).
There are also several pink-flowered ones: *M.* 'Galaxy' ♛, to 8m (25ft), with big purple-pink flowers; and *M.* 'Heaven Scent' ♛, 10m (30ft), with goblet-shaped flowers.
Forms of *M.* x *loebneri* reach about 8m (25ft). Among the best are 'Leonard Messel' ♛, with starry pink flowers, and 'Merrill' ♛, with profuse white flowers.
M. x *soulangeana* (p.18) is usually shrubby but 'Brozzonii' ♛ (white flowers) and 'Picture' (rich purple-pink and white flowers) are more tree-like. Both are 8m (25ft).

MAGNOLIA x *SOULANGEANA*

MAGNOLIA GRANDIFLORA 'GOLIATH' ♛

Summer-flowering magnolias
M. macrophylla grows to 10m (30ft) or more. It is broadly conical in habit with huge leaves and large but often sparse, creamy white flowers. *M. obovata* ♛ (syn. *M. hypoleuca*) also reaches 10m (30ft) or more. It has bold leaves and fragrant, crimson-centred flowers, often followed by red fruits in autumn. *M. virginiana* is usually smaller, with smaller flowers and glossy green leaves, blue-white beneath.

Evergreen magnolias
The evergreen magnolias have bold foliage and late flowers in summer and autumn. *M. delavayi*, to 8m (25ft), is often shrubby, with large deep blue-green leaves and big creamy white flowers. *M. grandiflora* is a large tree where summers are warm, but is usually less than 10m (30ft) in cooler areas. It has glossy dark green leaves and large, fragrant white flowers produced over a long period. 'Exmouth' ♛ is particularly hardy; 'Goliath' ♛ has broad leaves and very large flowers.

MALUS (CRAB APPLE)

Ornamental crab apples provide some of the toughest of all flowering trees growing in any reasonable soil. They are extremely hardy and capable of withstanding a good deal of exposure. In addition, they provide a profusion of flowers in late spring and early summer, often followed by variously coloured ornamental fruits. They are deciduous with a rounded to spreading habit, unless otherwise stated, and are ideal specimen trees for small gardens.

◫ ◊ ✲✲✲ H 8m (25ft)

Crab apples grown for flowers and fruit

Most crab apples are grown for their attractive flowers, which are often fragrant, and for their fruits.

M. 'Butterball' has apple-blossom-pink flowers on arching branches, followed by very profuse and persistent rounded fruits, which will mature from yellow flushed with red to golden yellow. **M. 'Donald Wyman'** has white flowers from pink buds and small, glossy red fruits. **M. florentina**, an unusual species, is broadly columnar in form, with attractively lobed leaves that turn to red and purple in autumn, white flowers, and small orange-red fruits. **M. floribunda** ♀ (Japanese crab apple) is compact with masses of

MALUS
'JOHN DOWNIE' ♀

flowers, red in bud opening to pale pink and eventually white, followed later by small yellow, slender-stalked fruits. **M. 'Golden Hornet'** ♀ (pp.8, 23) has white flowers from pink buds and showy golden yellow fruits. **M. hupehensis** ♀ is vigorous, to 10m (30ft) or more, with large white flowers from pink buds, and small, cherry-like red fruits. **M. 'John Downie'** ♀ is broadly conical in habit. The pink buds opening to white flowers are followed by very distinctive, conical red fruits that are flushed with yellow. **M. × magdeburgensis** has double pink flowers in large clusters. **M. 'Red Sentinel'** ♀ (p.9) is broadly conical, with white flowers and persistent glossy red fruits. **M. 'Snowdrift'** is compact with white flowers from pink buds and small, persistent, glossy orange-red fruits. **M. transitoria** ♀ has elegant foliage, small white flowers, and yellow, pea-sized fruits as the leaves turn yellow.

Crab apples grown for foliage

Some of the crab apples are grown particularly for their purple foliage. As with other purple-leaved trees, they colour best in full sun. **M. 'Liset'** has bronze-green leaves and purple-pink flowers in late spring followed by small purple-red fruits. **M. 'Profusion'** has bronze-purple leaves, red when young, later dark green, deep purple-pink flowers, and red-purple fruits. **M. 'Royalty'** has deep red-purple foliage, keeping its colour well and turning red in autumn. The flowers are red-purple, followed by small, deep purple fruits.

Crab apples grown for habit

Several crab apples combine ornamental flowers and fruit with an attractive habit. **M. 'Red Jade'** (p.60), to 4m

MALUS
FLORIBUNDA ♀

(12ft), has a mushroom-shaped head of arching shoots with pink-tinged, white flowers, then glossy red fruits. **M. 'Royal Beauty'** ♀ is smaller, weeping, with purple leaves and deep red-purple flowers. **M. tschonoskii** ♀ (p.15) is broadly columnar, to about 10m (30ft). It has bright orange and red autumn colour, small white flowers, tinged pink, and yellow fruits, flushed red. **M. 'Van Eseltine'** is narrowly columnar, to 8m (25ft) tall, and produces large, double, pink flowers.

MALUS 'SNOWDRIFT'

Nyssa sinensis ♀

N

Nyssa sinensis ♀
(Chinese tupelo)
This deciduous tree provides
colour at least as good as the
better-known *N. sylvatica* on
a tree only half the size. It
has large, dark green leaves,
which turn to brilliant shades
of orange, red, and yellow
in autumn. Often on several
stems, it has a rounded to
spreading habit. Requires
lime-free soil.
🖼 ◊ ✼✼✼ H 10m (30ft)

O

Oxydendrum arboreum
(Sorrel tree, Sourwood)
A deciduous, broadly conical
tree, which is sometimes
shrubby. In autumn, its long
bold, glossy dark green leaves
turn to shades of purple,
yellow, and red. Large,
arching clusters of small, urn-
shaped white flowers are
produced in late summer and
early autumn. It is best grown
in lime-free soil.
🖼 ◊ ✼✼✼ H 10m (30ft)

P

Photinia
These deciduous or evergreen,
mostly broadly columnar
trees are often grown for their
attractive leaves. They also
produce white flowers,
followed by colourful fruits.
P. davidiana, 8m (25ft) tall, is
evergreen and shrubby, with
arching branches. Bright red
fruits follow clusters of small
white flowers in summer and
may persist well into winter,
when occasional leaves turn
bright red before they fall.
The main ornamental feature
of the smaller evergreen *P. ×
fraseri*, 6m (20ft) tall, is its
young foliage, but it will
often produce small white
flowers in mid- and late
spring; 'Birmingham', 'Red
Robin' ♀, and 'Robusta' ♀ are
good forms with bright red
young leaves. The even
smaller *P. villosa* ♀, 5m (15ft)
tall, is deciduous and rounded
to spreading, sometimes
shrubby, and needs lime-free
soil. It has dark green leaves,
bronze when young, and
turning bright orange-red in

Oxydendrum arboreum

Photinia × fraseri
'Red Robin' ♀

autumn. Hawthorn-like white
flowers are borne in late
spring, followed by small,
bright red fruits.
🖼 ◊ ✼✼✼

Picea pungens
(Colorado spruce)
Best known in its blue-leaved
forms, such as f. *glauca* (p.26,
35) or 'Koster' ♀, this
evergreen conifer has stout
shoots, densely covered in
rigid, sharp-tipped, bright
silvery blue needles. It is best
grown in lime-free soil and is
narrowly columnar in shape.
Mature plants will bear pale
brown cones up to 10cm
(4in) long.
🖼 ◊ ✼✼✼ H 10m (30ft)

Picrasma quassioides
(Quassia tree)
This deciduous, broadly
columnar tree has dark green
divided leaves. Small green
flowers in early summer are
not very conspicuous. In
autumn, however, the elegant
leaves turn to orange, red,
and yellow, making it a
valuable foliage plant.
🖼 ◊ ✼✼✼ H 8m (25ft)

PRUNUS (CHERRIES, ALMONDS, PLUMS)

The cherries, almonds, and plums provide us with some of the best-loved spring-flowering trees. Most are small and rounded to spreading in habit; some provide additional interest, such as good autumn colour or attractive bark.
🌳 ◊ ✻✻✻ H 8–10m (25–30ft)

Flowering cherries
Some excellent early-flowering cherries include
P. 'Kursar' ♥ (deep pink);
P. 'Okame' ♥ (rich pink), also with good autumn colour; and P. 'Pandora' ♥ (pale pink), with bronze young leaves. P. sargentii ♥ has rich pink flowers and bronze young leaves, red in autumn.
P. × subhirtella 'Stellata' has pale pink flowers with pointed, star-like petals.
   There are some semi-double-flowered cherries, including P. 'Accolade' ♥ and the sometimes shrubby P. 'Hally Jolivette' (p.7), to 5m (15ft); both are pale pink.
   Double-flowered forms include P. × subhirtella 'Autumnalis' ♥ (white, pink-tinged in bud, p.21) and

PRUNUS × *SUBHIRTELLA* 'STELLATA'

'Autumnalis Rosea' ♥ (pink), both of which flower from autumn to early spring.

Japanese cherries
Recommended pink Japanese cherries include P. 'Kanzan' ♥ (double, deep pink) and P. 'Pink Perfection' ♥ (bright pink in large clusters). Recommended white-flowered forms include P. 'Mount Fuji' ♥ (syn. P. 'Shirotae', double); P. 'Shôgetsu' ♥ (large, double, with frilled edges); and P. 'Taihaku' ♥ (Great white cherry), with very large flowers.
   The very late P. 'Shirofugen' ♥ has double flowers with purple-pink buds opening to white, then fading to purple-pink again amid bronze young foliage. P. 'Ukon' ♥ has semi-double, creamy flowers, flushed green and pink.

Cherries grown for bark
Cherries with ornamental bark include P. maackii (Manchurian cherry), with golden-brown peeling bark and small white flowers in spring; 'Amber Beauty' has amber bark. P. serrula ♥ (Tibetan cherry, p.23) has glossy, mahogany-red bark and white flowers.

Cherries for ornamental habit
Good upright cherries include the narrowly columnar P. 'Amanogawa' ♥, with single to semi-double, pink flowers, and P. sargentii RANCHO, with pink flowers and good autumn colour. The broadly columnar P. 'Spire' ♥ has pink flowers and attractive orange and red autumn colour.
   There are also a number of weeping forms: P. 'Kiku-shidare-zakura' (syn. P. 'Cheal's Weeping') only reaches 2.5m (8ft), and has clusters of large, double pink flowers before the leaves emerge.

PRUNUS 'UKON' ♥

P. pendula (p.37) has slender pendulous shoots. Good pink forms include 'Pendula Rosea' ♥ (p.14) and the double 'Pendula Rubra' ♥.
P. × yedoensis ♥ has arching branches, to 6m (20ft), and an attractive mass of pale pink flowers, fading to white, in early spring.

Almonds and plums
Several forms of P. cerasifera (Cherry plum) have purple foliage, but their small, profuse flowers, borne in late winter and early spring, pink in 'Nigra' ♥, white in 'Pissardii', are their best asset.
P. dulcis (Almond) has very early, large, pink or white flowers. P. mume (Japanese apricot) has forms that produce attractive white to deep pink flowers in early spring.

PRUNUS SARGENTII ♥

PINUS DENSIFLORA
'UMBRACULIFERA'

Pinus
Pines are evergreen conifers.
P. bungeana (Lacebark pine)
has bark that flakes, leaving a
patchwork of cream, grey,
and green. It is slow growing,
columnar or bushy headed,
and may reach a height of
10m (30ft). *P. densiflora*
'Umbraculifera' makes a
dense, rounded head of
slender grey-green needles.
Forms of *P. sylvestris* (Scots
pine) include 'Aurea' ♀, with
bright yellow winter foliage,
which may exceed 10m (30ft).
'Fastigiata' is narrow, to 8m
(25ft) tall, whereas 'Watereri'
is rounded, with blue-grey
foliage, to nearly 10m (30ft).
🔲 ◊ ✻✻✻

Pittosporum tenuifolium
Evergreen, broadly columnar
tree (*p.35*) with small, wavy-
edged leaves borne on dark
shoots. Deep purple-red,
honey-scented flowers open in
late spring and early summer.
'Abbotsbury Gold' has leaves
blotched yellow-green in the
centre; 'Purpureum' has
glossy purple foliage; 'Silver
Queen' has grey-green, white-

edged leaves; and 'Warnham
Gold' has pale green leaves
that are soft yellow in winter.
🔲 ◊ ✻✻ H 10m (30ft)

Pyrus calleryana
'Chanticleer' (Pear)
Narrow and fast-growing,
deciduous tree with glossy
foliage, red-purple in late
autumn and winter. Small
white flowers appear in late
winter and early spring, and
small russet-brown fruits may
be produced in autumn.
🔲 ◊ ✻✻✻ H 10m (30ft)

Pyrus salicifolia 'Pendula'
(Weeping silver pear)
This deciduous tree (*p.21*)
makes a mound of pendulous
shoots bearing silvery grey,
willow-like leaves. Creamy
white flowers open in spring.
🔲 ◊ ✻✻✻ H 5m (15ft)

Q

Quercus
(Oak)
There are several small
evergreen oaks that make
valuable foliage plants.
Q. glauca is broadly

PITTOSPORUM TENUIFOLIUM

ROBINIA 'IDAHO'

columnar and bushy, growing
to about 6m (20ft) tall, with
red buds and glossy green
leaves, bronze in spring.
Q. myrsinifolia is rounded,
with dark green, taper-
pointed leaves, bronze when
young. *Q. phillyreoides* is an
often shrubby tree with
leathery dark green leaves.
🔲 ◊ ✻✻✻ H 10m (30ft)

R

Rhus chinensis 'September
Beauty' (Sumach)
Deciduous, rounded to
broadly columnar tree, with
leaves that turn orange-red in
autumn and clusters of small,
creamy white flowers in late
summer and early autumn.
🔲 ◊ ✻✻✻ H 6m (20ft)

Rhus typhina
(Stag's horn sumach)
This deciduous tree is late
into leaf but early to colour in
autumn, turning orange and
red on velvety shoots. Bears
red fruit clusters in autumn.
The sap may irritate the skin.
Suckers freely.
🔲 ◊ ✻✻✻ H 5m (15ft)

Robinia

These are often thorny trees. **R. 'Idaho'** is spreading, to 12m (40ft), with fragrant flowers in late spring. **R. × margarettae 'Pink Cascade'**, with drooping clusters of deep purple-pink flowers in late spring, reaches 10m (30ft). Avoid most forms of the common **R. pseudoacacia** if you want a small tree (even the popular **'Frisia'** ♀ reaches at least 15m/50ft). However, the more compact **'Umbraculifera'** (Mop-headed acacia), grown for its dense rounded head, will reach only about 6m (20ft). **R. × slavinii 'Hillieri'** ♀ is graceful with arching shoots and lilac-pink flower clusters.

🔲 ◊ ✳✳✳

S

Salix

(Willow)

There are several willows that are suitable for growing in small gardens (vigorous kinds should be planted far from buildings, since their invasive root systems can damage drains). Forms of **S. alba** (White willow), such as **'Britzensis'** ♀ (*p.57*) and subsp. **vitellina** ♀, are grown for their coloured winter stems. Pollard them for brighter shoots and to keep them small (*see p.57*). **S. babylonica 'Tortuosa'** ♀ (Dragon's claw willow), to 9m (28ft), has twisted stems. **S. caprea 'Kilmarnock'** ♀ is 2m (6ft) or less. Stout shoots weep almost to the ground and, in late winter to spring, they bear silvery catkins that turn yellow as the stamens emerge. **S. 'Erythroflexuosa'** is

SORBUS (WHITEBEAM, ROWAN)

*SORBUS
ALNIFOLIA*

This genus is often broadly divided into two groups, the whitebeams and the rowans. Both provide a good range of small deciduous trees offering white flowers, attractive berries in many colours, and often excellent autumn colour.

🔲 ◊ ✳✳✳ H 10m (30ft)

Whitebeams

The whitebeams, mostly rounded to spreading, have toothed or lobed leaves. They are mostly tough trees, good in dry soils and urban sites. **S. alnifolia** (Korean mountain ash) is conical, later rounded, sometimes up to 20m (60ft), with leaves orange to red in autumn, and red berries. **S. aria** has glossy dark green leaves, and red berries. Its forms include **'Lutescens'** ♀, with silvery young foliage, and **'Majestica'** ♀, with very large leaves. **S. intermedia** is dense and rounded and may be slightly larger than **S. aria**; it has dark green leaves and bright red fruits. **S. × thuringiaca 'Fastigiata'** is similar to **S. aria**, but is dense and broadly conical.

Rowans

The rowans, broadly conical, are more graceful than the whitebeams, with leaves cut into numerous leaflets. They

generally prefer a moister soil and include the best species for autumn colour. **S. americana** (American mountain ash) has large clusters of red berries, and yellow or red autumn foliage. **S. aucuparia** (Mountain ash, Rowan, *p.31*) is similar, with forms such as **'Aspleniifolia'**, with finely cut leaves, and **'Fructu Luteo'** ♀, with yellow berries. **S. cashmiriana** ♀ is a small tree, to 8m (25ft) tall, with elegant foliage and white or pink flowers and large white berries, pink when immature. **S. commixta** has red autumn colour and bright orange-red fruits; **'Embley'** ♀ is a particularly good form. **S. hupehensis** ♀, to 8m (25ft), is among the best rowans for white fruits, with blue-green leaves, red in autumn; var. **obtusa** ♀ has pink berries. **S. 'Joseph Rock'** ♀ is broadly columnar, and produces yellow fruits and orange, red, and purple autumn colour. **S. sargentiana** ♀ has bold leaves, red in autumn, and large heads of small red berries, whereas **S. scalaris** ♀ is spreading, with fern-like foliage, purple in autumn, and red berries. **S. vilmorinii** ♀ is smaller, reaching only 5m (15ft) tall, and produces red berries that turn pink, then later white.

*SORBUS
SCALARIS* ♀

a rounded to spreading, deciduous tree, to 5m (15ft) tall, with contorted shoots, bright orange-pink in winter. *S. integra* 'Hakuro-nishiki' (*p.15*) is a rounded to spreading, deciduous shrub, usually grown as a dwarf tree, to 1.5m (5ft) tall. It has white young foliage that becomes speckled with dark green.
🔲 ◊ ✽✽✽

Sophora japonica 'Pendula'
(Japanese pagoda tree)
This weeping, deciduous tree has a dense head of twisted branches, from which long hanging shoots cascade to the ground. Slightly fragrant, white pea-flowers, produced in large clusters, open in late summer, but only at the end of very hot summers.
🔲 ◊ ✽✽✽ H 3m (10ft) or more

Stewartia
These are deciduous or evergreen trees grown for their attractive white flowers, often peeling bark, and good autumn colour. They require lime-free soil. *S. ovata*, 5m (15ft) tall, is often shrubby, with large white flowers in

STYRAX JAPONICUS

SYRINGA RETICULATA

summer. The young leaves are red, then green, turning red once again in autumn. The larger *S. pseudocamellia* ♀, 10m (30ft) tall, is broadly columnar with large white flowers in midsummer. Older trunks have red-brown, tan, and grey peeling bark. The dark green leaves turn shades of orange and red in autumn.
🔲 ◊ ✽✽✽

Styrax
These graceful deciduous or evergreen trees produce fragrant, pendulous flowers. *S. japonicus* (Japanese snowbell, *p.10*) is rounded to spreading, 8m (25ft) tall, and needs lime-free soil. Bell-shaped white flowers hang on slender stalks in early summer. Glossy green leaves turn yellow or red in autumn. 'Pink Chimes' produces pale pink flowers. *S. obassia* ♀ (Fragrant snowbell) is more upright, and is also larger, to 12m (25ft) tall. It has bold, rounded leaves and drooping spikes of white flowers in early and midsummer. Does best in lime-free soil.
✳ ◊ ✽✽✽

Syringa reticulata
(Japanese tree lilac)
Deciduous, rounded to spreading tree, which bears small fragrant white flowers opening in large heads in summer. 'Ivory Lace' is compact and free-flowering.
🔲 ◊ ✽✽✽ H 10m (30ft)

Syringa vulgaris
(Common lilac)
This spreading shrub may become tree-like with age. It bears heart-shaped leaves and very fragrant single or double lilac flowers in late spring and early summer.
🔲 ◊ ✽✽✽ H 7m (22ft)

T

Taxus baccata
(Common yew)
Evergreen, rounded to spreading conifer with dark green foliage and purple-brown bark. 'Dovastonii Aurea' ♀ is male, to about 5m (15ft) tall but wide-spreading, with drooping shoots and leaves with yellow edges. 'Fastigiata' ♀ (Irish yew) is female, with dense upright

THUJA KORAIENSIS

shoots and red fruits.
'**Fastigiata Aureomarginata**' ♀
is similar, but is male, grows
only to 5m (15ft), and has
yellow-edged leaves.
'**Standishii**', to 1.5m (5ft), is a
miniature selection of
'Fastigiata', with yellow
leaves. The foliage and seeds
of all yews are toxic.
◉ ◊ ✽✽✽ H 10m (30ft)

Thuja koraiensis
(Korean arborvitae)
A dense, bushy, shrubby
or narrowly conical, slow-
growing tree with dark green
aromatic foliage, bright
silvery white beneath.
◨ ◊ ✽✽✽ H 10m (30ft)

Thuja occidentalis
(White cedar)
This small, narrowly
columnar evergreen conifer
with scale-like leaves has
several forms: '**Europa Gold**',
with bright yellow foliage;
'**Holmstrup**' ♀, which is
compact with vertical sprays
of rich green foliage; and
'**Smaragd**' ♀, which is slow
growing and narrow, with
bright green foliage.
◨ ◊ ✽✽✽ H 6m (20ft)

Trachycarpus fortunei ♀
(Chinese windmill palm,
Chusan palm)
Evergreen, narrowly
columnar tree with large
leaves deeply cut into long,
slender lobes and borne in a
cluster on an unbranched
fibrous trunk. Large clusters
of tiny creamy flowers emerge
in early summer.
◨ ◊ ✽✽✽ H 10m (30ft)

Trochodendron aralioides
Evergreen, broadly columnar
tree with leathery dark green,
taper-pointed leaves and
clusters of bright green
flowers at the ends of the
shoots in spring. This unusual
specimen is suitable for a
woodland garden, and
requires acid soil to thrive.
◨◉ ◊ ✽✽ H 10m (30ft)

Tsuga heterophylla
'**Laursen's Column**'
This evergreen conifer, a form
of the normally large Western
hemlock, has a narrowly
columnar habit, making it
excellent as a feature tree.
The dark green leaves have
white bands beneath. It grows
well in sun or shade in most
soils, including chalk.
◉◨ ✽✽✽ H 8m (25ft)

U

Ulmus
(Elm)
Deciduous trees, grown
mainly for their foliage and
habit. Some forms are
excellent for small gardens.
U. glabra '**Camperdownii**'
(Camperdown elm), 8m (25ft)
tall, makes a dense mound of
shoots, weeping to the
ground. Produces twisted

branches and toothed, dark
matt green leaves. *Ulmus
minor* '**Dampieri Aurea**', 10m
(30ft) tall, is broadly conical,
with golden leaves.
◨ ✽✽✽

V

Viburnum prunifolium
(Black haw)
An upright, broadly columnar
deciduous tree, sometimes
shrubby, with dark green
leaves often turning orange or
red in autumn. Domed heads
of white flowers in late spring
are followed by pink, later
blue-black, fruits.
◨ ◊ ✽✽✽ H 5m (15ft)

Viburnum sieboldii
Compact and spreading,
deciduous shrub, which may
be trained as a tree by
removing the lower branches
as it develops to give a clear
stem. It has bold, glossy dark
green leaves and produces
large heads of small white
flowers in late spring, later
followed by glossy red fruits
that turn black.
◨◨ ◊ ✽✽✽ H 6m (20ft)

TRACHYCARPUS FORTUNEI ♀

VIBURNUM PRUNIFOLIUM

INDEX

Page numbers in *italics*
indicate illustrations.

ACKNOWLEDGMENTS

Picture research Emily Hedges

Index Hilary Bird

Illustrations Karen Cochrane

Dorling Kindersley would like to thank:
All staff at the RHS, in particular Susanne
Mitchell, Karen Wilson, and Barbara Haynes
at Vincent Square; Sir Harold Hillier Gardens
and Arboretum; John Hillier. Thanks also to
Helen Bracey for design assistance and Lesley
Malkin for editorial help.

The Royal Horticultural Society
To learn more about the work of the
Society, visit the RHS on the Internet at
www.rhs.org.uk. Information includes news of
events around the country, a horticultural
database, international plant registers, results
of plant trials, and membership details.

Photography
The publisher would like to thank the
following for their kind permission to
reproduce their photographs:
(key: t=top; b=below; l=left; r=right)

Dr. Mike Dirr: 67bl
Garden Picture Library: Mark Bolton 40;
John Glover 10l (Valley Gardens, Windsor),
13; Jerry Pavia 30; J.S. Sira 37l (The Coppice,
Surrey)
John Glover: 8bl (Old Place Farm, Kent), 22b,
25tr, 29t
Jerry Harpur: 10r (Helen Yemm), 26r, 31t, 34
(Little Malvern Court)
Marcus Harpur: 22t
Andrew Lawson: 21b, 28r, 41
Marianne Majerus: 18r (designer: Penny
Snell), 36 (designer: Tessa Hobbs)
S&O Mathews: 8tr, 9, 11, 14, 15r, 32, 33
Clive Nichols: 12, 15l (The Dingle, Welshpool,
Wales), 16 (Osler Road, Oxford), 17t, 17b
(designer: C. Caplin), 18l (White Windows,
Hampshire), 19 (Little Court, Crawley,
Hampshire), 20 (designer: Jill Billington), 21t
(The Anchorage, Kent), 23t and b, 35bl
(designer: Thomasina Tarling), 38t (Ling
Beeches, Yorkshire), 39 (designers: Mr. and
Mrs. D. Terry)

Cover photography:
S&O Mathews: back tl; **Clive Nichols:** back b;
Jerry Harpur: front tl; **S&O Mathews:** front r